DISGRUNTLED AMERICA

A Voice for the Silent Majority

by

Darren C Bowman

authorHOUSE®

AuthorHouse™
1663 Liberty Drive, Suite 200
Bloomington, IN 47403
www.authorhouse.com
Phone: 1-800-839-8640

First published by AuthorHouse 1/9/2008

ISBN: 978-1-4343-4198-3 (sc)

Printed in the United States of America
Bloomington, Indiana

This book is printed on acid-free paper.

FOREWORD

If I may be so bold, I will begin writing this book with the help of a quote of a great American from many years ago as he began a literary masterpiece: "Perhaps the sentiments contained in the following pages, are not yet sufficiently fashionable to procure them general favor; a long habit of not thinking a thing Wrong, gives it a superficial appearance of being Right, and raises a formidable outcry in the defense of custom" (Thomas Paine, *Common Sense*, February 14, 1776). There are many things the American people have been convinced are not wrong, and they have been left with the attitude that they must be right.

People accept things as right because so many others do, and merely reply, "That's the way we have always done it," with no actual consideration as to whether it is right or whether it is wrong. This is what Thomas Paine was trying to say to the people of 1776 so many years ago.

The greatness of this nation is not measured by the greatness of its government but on the greatness of its citizens. It is every citizen's responsibility and duty to ensure the preservation of this nation, and not only must we as a people preserve the nation, but we must also preserve the ideals of this nation. Unfortunately, for about the last thirty to forty years, the general population has not educated itself enough to really understand the problems and even, in some cases, the dangers that face this great nation. The reason for this? Too many people do not understand the Constitution. The very document that protects them, it is the keystone for a free nation and a free people. The Constitution dictates and protects the rights of the citizenry by limiting the power of the government. Let us adjust that last statement. The Constitution dictates and protects the rights of the citizenry by limiting the power of the government and the leaders of the government. Now imagine if you would, having an alarm in your home but not knowing its purpose or how it operates. Sounds silly? It would be useless and not offer much protection without your knowing the much-needed information on how it should operate. Yet, the rights and protections afforded the people by the Constitution are as unknown to them as having that alarm, but their own ignorance has prevented them from knowing how to make it work. The only things many understand are that the Constitution was written a long time ago by the founding fathers and that it has something to do with rights. A slightly larger number of people may know what a few rights of Americans are, by what they may have seen or heard on television shows. Most young men and women base their rights on their age: when they become seventeen years of age, they have the right to go to R-rated movies; when they turn eighteen years of age, they can buy cigarettes and vote; when they turn twenty-one years of age, they can get married without consent and purchase alcohol. Most will begin their adult lives totally ignorant of the vehicle that gives them the opportunities that lie before them. They only know that they are able to do what they want because this is a free country. They do not know why they are free or how they are free. They do not know how expensive freedom is, or who is paying, or who has paid the expense for their freedom. Nor do they know that their responsibility is to ensure that the same freedom they now exercise is around for their children and grandchildren to exercise as well. It is easy to complain about that of which you have no knowledge, and many of these young men and women will become complainers and be disgruntled, like many young men and women before them—all because, they do not know the role of government, dictated by the Constitution. They do not know how the different branches of government are supposed to work. Without this knowledge, they cannot help themselves by electing honest and forthright representatives, senators, and even presidents to lead this country. They do not comprehend that the Constitution was written for them, not the politicians. There are many politicians that want them to remain ignorant. They pander to the working class as if they share our burden. Their children go to private schools while they attend country clubs. Are they really helping their children with homework or just trying to act like an average Joe? Have you ever bumped into a politician at the grocery store or at the auto mechanic's shop (other than when they were campaigning)? Why, because most of them have some hired hand to do those chores. They probably could not tell you what a carton of eggs or a gallon of milk costs. That does not seem to stop them from this continuous barrage of pandering to the working class, telling us they know that our life is tough and they feel our pain. There is nothing wrong with having private tutors and using the benefits of one's wealth for education or simply personal satisfaction. Many of us would hire private tutors for our children if it were financially feasible. Let us not begrudge any person the spoils of hard work, success, or inheritance. There is no constructive reason to engage in class warfare; this only creates more discontent. Why, then, do politicians pretend to be someone they are not? Is it because they have attempted to demonize the wealthy as one of the major ills of this country, while at the same time going to great lengths only to make a feeble attempt to try to conceal from the public that they are members of the upper class? Many candidates portray themselves as the working class, or as advocates of the working class, in a desperate attempt to secure your vote. Many have the sole intent of holding onto power in order to control you with your own money. It is time we stood up, called them by name, and held them accountable. We need to realize we have a responsibility to ourselves and the nation to take part, as a whole. We are their bosses. Do not let them fill your mind with all this talk about not having time to get involved. (They always want you to take time to vote for them.) We live in the world of microwaves, automatic washers, dryers, self-cleaning ovens, frost-free refrigerators, vacuum cleaners, and superstores. Yet, people still say there is not enough time to pay attention to their own children, let alone politics and how this country is run. Well, that is what some politicians want you to think, so they keep making speeches about how tough it is to raise a family and work. Although that may be true, many politicians want you to think you are helpless without their assistance. They try to create dependence from you on the federal government. They create programs that promote this dependence, leaving the recipient to feel that they cannot fulfill their responsibilities to their family and their employer without the help of government. It is human nature to think your job is more difficult than the next person's, that your responsibilities are more difficult than the neighbor's. Let us take a close look at keeping the house and doing daily chores. In my childhood, it was exhausting during visits to my grandmother and watching her throughout the week. She did have milk and eggs delivered to the back door, but that is where the simplicity of her chores ended. On Monday, she started the laundry. That consisted of putting the clothes in an old wringer washer. When they were finished washing, she put them through the wringer and took them to the clothesline and hung them up, then proceeded with the next load. She had to remain there until all the clothes were done. When she took the clothes off the line, she put them in baskets to be ironed the next day. After doing that, she started dinner for the family, and she cooked everything from scratch, even the macaroni and cheese. You see, there were no thirty-minute dinners. When she went to the market on Wednesday, she went to the butcher and placed her order in the morning; then it was off to the bakery to do the same. Afterwards, we went to a store and got staple goods and other supplies. Then we made a return trip, stopping back by the bakery and butcher shop. This was all done on foot, with no car; you see; my grandmother in her ninety-seven years of life never once drove a car. When we arrived home, it was time to start the family dinner again. It should be noted, all the dishes were done by hand. All these chores that my grandmother used to do with pride and joy never kept her from fulfilling other, more fun times with her family. There should be serious doubts that many would want to switch places with her. We actually have more time to do the things we want than ever before. My uncle's chores, after he got home from work, included working in the garden with a mule. Yet, he took me and my cousins swimming and fishing when time permitted and all the chores were done. Therefore, if you are one of these people that feel sorry for themselves about having too much to do, perhaps, you should stop reading now. You will get no mercy from me, as I was a single father of four boys for several years from the time my twin boys were fourteen months old. Yes, it required me to work full-time, and I managed to utilize two, day care centers. Yes, it was tiring, but that would not keep me from fulfilling my responsibilities or duties. We need to educate ourselves and stay involved; it is the only way we can take back our government and ensure that our freedom is preserved for many generations ahead. This can and must be accomplished. Many of you have seen your parents work their butts off to put food on the table and probably look back and admire them for it. What kind of person are you? Perhaps they helped build your character and work ethic more than you realize. Do not let someone who does not even know you, who has no idea about your daily life, convince you that they are looking out for your best interest, without closely investigating what they really stand for.

Many of today's politicians are hoping you do not change and continue to pay little attention to your elected officials. These politicians are from both sides of the political aisle. It always amazes me when a politician is trying to explain a position and seems to be talking down to the electorate. You probably have noticed it yourselves. You probably get the same thing from your doctor. The only difference is, you and your doctor are one-on-one, and you can say, "Time out—you have got to explain it a little better." A politician is usually talking to a large group of people, and you do not have the luxury of one-on-one dialogue. If you could slow them down and make them speak in non-technical language, they probably could not explain half of what they said. When they talk about budgets and taxes, it would be nice if they would talk in working-family lingo. Nevertheless, they do not; either they do not know how, or they know the people would never go for half of their ridiculous ideas. In the early days of this country, representatives were typically well-respected members of their communities. They were elected based on their integrity and devotion to their respective communities. These communities sought out individuals they could trust to take their views and opinions to Philadelphia. Let it not be forgotten, these were also very brave men who, if captured, could be executed for treason against England, as there were rewards placed on those participating in forwarding the independence movement. If one possesses the necessary intestinal fortitude to risk one's life, then having the courage to be honest and forthright comes very easily. To exemplify this courage, you need only to look at John Hancock, who, having the largest recognizable signature on the Declaration of Independence, when he signed his name, commented "The British Ministry can read that name without spectacles: let them double their reward." (In today's standards, that would be like giving the king the finger.) How refreshing it would be to have congressional representatives, regardless of party affiliation, with that type of resolve and character.

Unfortunately, many of the politicians are spineless cowards who do not have the courage to talk straight to the American people. These people do not deserve to hold their offices. In many regards, it is an absolute disgrace to those brave souls that held that office before them.

TABLE OF CONTENTS

Disgruntlement #1:
THE MEDIA

The mainstream media has its hands very dirty. Many people in the mainstream are guilty of perpetuating ignorance by use of political correctness. Some do this because of their own political viewpoints; some do it because they are ignorant themselves. They base their knowledge on what other people have told them is in the Constitution, the Declaration of Independence, important Supreme Court decisions, and a multitude of other important documents, letters, and publications, instead of reading and researching said documents for their own education. Regardless of why, the press has, in many instances, betrayed its role to the nation, granted it by the U.S. Constitution. The media has provided plenty of editorial comment, as was provided for and intended by the Constitution. They have not, however, fulfilled their duty, nor have they honored or respected the intent that the press be the disseminators of truth and facts without reference to their own viewpoints. Although the media may disagree, they are certainly entitled to have opposing viewpoints. However, when they intermingle an opinionated view not based entirely on facts, or on facts at all, with actuality is when they betray the truth. The intent was for the press to print dissenting viewpoints and editorials without repercussion from the government. That right should be coveted, respected, and protected to the utmost ability. The press also has a responsibility to the truth and facts without bias. The founding fathers knew that in order to have a free and educated electorate, there must be an avenue for discovery of what are truth, fact, and otherwise viewpoint. This avenue could only be achieved by having a free press. To accommodate this, on December 15, 1791, they ratified the Bill of Rights, in which the first amendment states: "Congress shall make no law respecting an establishment of religion, or prohibiting the free exercise thereof: or abridging the freedom of speech, or of the press, or the right of the people peaceably to assemble, and to petition the

Government for a redress of grievances." There is a thin line between reporting and editorializing; the amendment cited here is absolutely word for word, of what it states; this is an undeniable fact. Editorials are created when we try to decipher what it means, or when we try to re-write what it means, by inserting phrases like "freedom of expression" and "separation of church and state." The *fact* is that you will *not* find anywhere in the U.S. Constitution any such phrases or references regarding those erroneous insertions. It is interpretations and viewpoints not engraved by the chisel of fact that have confused and disgruntled the good people of this great nation. They make decisions sometimes based on falsehood, perpetuated by those who care for the people only as a means for power and wealth. If the people educate themselves properly and thoroughly, these power-mongers will lose control over the electorate. We must remember, we have been granted an enormous amount of power as citizens of this country. We must learn to use that power and wield it without malice to the truth. Let us reclaim our nation and our values from the people who would try to strip us of them. The first step is to determine how we have lost our authority by surrendering it voluntarily. The second step will be to learn how to read between the lines when some would have us duped into believing they are looking out for our best interest. Always remember:

'….that this nation, under God, shall have a new birth of freedom—and that government of the people, by the people, for the people, shall not perish from the earth."

For those of you that read this last sentence and thought it was from the U.S. Constitution, you are wrong. It is the last passage of the Gettysburg Address, of course written by President Abraham Lincoln. Thus, the lessons begin.

You must first ask yourself, "What ulterior motive would the media have for perpetuating political correctness and liberal bias?" You need look no further than the U.S. Constitution and how the media for their own agenda have exploited it. What is their agenda, you ask? The answer is influence, power, and money. In the foreword, you will find a comment that the U.S. citizens have been granted an enormous amount of power. The Bill of Rights secures that power for the people by preventing the government from depriving the individual of the very rights that were so eloquently stated by a document preceding the U.S. Constitution, which we as a people hold just as dear: the Declaration of Independence. "We hold these truths to be self-evident, that all men are created equal, that they are endowed by their Creator with certain unalienable Rights, that these are Life, Liberty and the pursuit of Happiness. —That to secure these rights, Governments are instituted among Men, deriving their powers from the consent of the governed. That whenever any Form of Government becomes destructive of the ends, it is the Right of the People to alter or abolish it and to institute new government...." The founding fathers knew that in order for the people of this great country to consent to how they would be governed, they must first know what they were consenting to. This was to be the media's role; as we documented in the foreword, the First Amendment of the U.S. Constitution addressed it. The founding fathers purposely listed a group of rights within the First Amendment in a specific order, one right listed before the others in a cascading nature to protect each segment of the First Amendment. To demonstrate this, we must revisit the Declaration of Independence. The founding fathers truly believed that God granted freedom and liberty. They used that premise in order to declare independence from England—that the Creator (God) was above governments. It was God who granted all people unalienable rights, not the government. Thus, the First Amendment prevents the government from establishing a religion.

(First Amendment, first phrase: "Congress shall make no law respecting the establishment of religion.") If the government had been able to establish a religion, the government could then dictate the doctrine of that religion, altering the unalienable rights granted by the Creator and recognized by the founding fathers.

(First Amendment, second phrase: "or prohibit the free exercise thereof.") Many kingdoms, dictatorships, and empires sought and still seek to this day to abolish religion and their peoples' right to worship as they please. They do this for the stated reason in the Declaration of Independence: that our Creator granted and meant for us to be entitled to Life, Liberty, and the pursuit of Happiness, and if a government seeks to quash these rights, the people have a right to overthrow the government and install a government that will protect and support these rights. Allowing people to believe our Creator is above government and has granted us unalienable rights is not conducive to running an oppressive style of government.

(First Amendment, third phrase: "or abridging the freedom of speech.") If someone disagreed with actions of the government or government official, they would not be quelled by the powers of the government or government official. This is a way to challenge the thinking and the actions of our leaders without worry of prosecution. The freedom of speech does not necessarily have to deal only with facts and proven truth, but must also allow ideas without proof or merit. It must allow for editorial and speculation without an ounce of legitimacy. Provided, of course, it is not libelous towards an individual, company, or corporation.

(First Amendment, fourth phrase: "or of the press.") The importance of these four words in the constitution cannot be ignored. How else would people be informed *en masse* of possible travesties against truth or an individual or people? How would they know of events going on around them and in other places? Without these four words, an oppressive government would be strengthened by keeping the people ignorant of facts and truth. This is where the U.S. Constitution provided a role for the press. This role was not provided to enhance the sale of the news, but rather to ensure the electorate stayed educated and aware. In reporting, the press has a duty to the truth and facts and must be allowed to pursue this duty without restraint from the government. (National security is an obvious exception.) Only in editorials should the press follow the same standard as an individual exercising freedom of speech.

(First Amendment, fifth phrase: "and of the right of the people peaceably to assemble.") Thus, after being informed and educated by the press and the people that have spoken out, the citizens have a right to assemble and march and protest against the government, or even a company or corporation, without recourse.

(First amendment, sixth phrase: "and to petition the government for a redress of grievances.") Before or after such assemblies, citizens may either sign their names to a grievance or petition without fear of torment from the government.

As you can see, the First Amendment was methodically thought out and phrased in just the right order to prevent the government from ever becoming oppressive. Another way of thinking about people's rights is thinking of them as government preventions. The First Amendment, as well as the rest of the Bill of Rights and the entire U.S. Constitution, was written to protect the people from the government. The founding fathers were wise enough to know they could not possibly see into the future; that is why they left us with the marvelous documents that would protect this wonderful nation. The task of protecting this nation was not simply having a strong military, but also a free and open society, a society of thinking men and women having an avenue to share their ideas. The founding fathers knew that in order to accomplish this, the media would play an instrumental role. Why did I write in the foreword that many in the media have betrayed their role and duty? Well, let us consider again the founding fathers. Each of the founding fathers was religious; some were of the same denomination. They affirmed their religious belief in the Declaration of Independence when they stated that rights were granted by God. Yet, they wrote the First amendment not only to hamstring future elected officials, but also themselves. They were compelled by the duty to an idea and would not let their personal views influence their resolve. They could not be bought with money or personal glory. In fact, they made it rather difficult to change the U.S. Constitution. However, the media is not so constrained; they have only to change their ideals as generations pass. This, in contrast, is rather easy to do. Many have abandoned their role, which was to be neutral in politics and religion. Many are influenced greatly by money and personal glory. How many times have you heard that the press prints what sells papers? There is big money in the media from the big markets of New York, Chicago, and Los Angeles. If you look at the political registration of the markets, you will find they are liberal Meccas, Democrat strongholds. Is it any wonder the media tries to appeal to these areas with a more liberal slant on the national television news anchors and news programs? Of course not. If you cannot see this or will not see this, you are kidding yourself. The considerable pandering that happens in these markets is shameful. Audiences are receptive in these markets to the liberal slant of the media. In the Deep South and Midwest rural areas, people are more receptive to a conservative slant. Truth and facts are not something that should be processed and canned, then sold to the public. They are something that must be delivered straight, without additives, even if they are not what the particular market wants to hear. People are more prone to listen to you if you are telling them something they want to hear. (Just ask every candidate that runs for office.) For media outlets to make money, they must sell advertising. The cost of such advertising is based on market share; the more people that listen = more revenue in advertising money. (If you are still not willing to believe this, then try a little experiment. Disagree with some of your friends on a particular subject. If you get answers like "I don't want to talk about it anymore" or even the cold shoulder for a few days, then imagine if your were a television channel that could be changed or a newspaper that stayed at the newsstand.) You may ask yourself, "How and why do the media slant their political coverage to the more liberal side?" First, let us deal with the how. The media understands how people receive and interpret the news, as well as the recipients' tendencies and habits. The news is then structured in a way to take every advantage of these tendencies and habits to result in a favorable view to whichever side the media wishes to support. For instance, most people that get a newspaper will not read an entire article; that is one of the reasons articles are continued on subsequent pages of a newspaper— in many cases, several pages later. The media will simply bury the opposing facts or arguments on the latter pages because they know that in many cases, the continuation will never be read. You may have heard of the media "playing hardball." If you have not, this is where the media will try to ask every conceivable question to stump or confuse a particular person on his/her views or ideas. The fact is the media also plays softball with some people asking only questions that will be easy to answer and paint the individual in a good light. There are also times when an individual actually receives the questions that will be asked by the interviewer in advance so that they might prepare the answers. Sometimes, you can watch a news interview where they allow a particular person to reverse their previous statements and never question them on it. Even though they may have a previous answer or statement on record that is in total conflict with what they are now stating, the media never makes the person accountable for the reversal. (I would like to see an interview where the interviewer questioned a candidate, and then when the candidate says something that is not true, the interviewer would flash back to a video with the candidate's contradicting statement.) People should be allowed to change their minds. However, if they are a public figure and they have reversed course on a position, they should explain why. The media is willing in many cases to try to sweep it under the rug if your political leanings are in line with their own. Now, we must ask ourselves, why is the media more liberal than conservative? Consider first that in this context, *liberal* means a broad interpretation of the Constitution. Remember in the First Amendment the freedom of the press. We acknowledge that the First Amendment grants an enormous amount of power. Putting the two together, it is only natural that the liberal view which the press takes and supports means they are supporting a broader amount of power for themselves. They want the population to lean to the liberal side because this means more influence for them, and with influence comes even more power money and wealth. The money in the media has unfortunately corrupted the original intent of the founding fathers. Obviously, the founding fathers knew the media would make money distributing the news, and in a capitalistic society, that is great. However, the media was also supposed to help reinforce the fairness wherein both sides of an equation were given equal coverage and let all people be heard equally; if they are fools, then better we know who they are. Then we will be making our individual judgment—something we are entitled to do, each and every one of us. I, personally, do not need the media to help me with my opinion. I only need the facts of the matter. The media has grown very powerful over the years—so powerful that, like the story in Genesis of Cain and Abel, the media must weaken and destroy its brother as well. Yes, born of the same pen, the same idea, in the same amendment, was freedom of religion and freedom of the press. Religion has a profound influence over some people—more so than the media. As Cain could not let himself be overshadowed by Abel, the media has done its best not to be overshadowed by religion, especially Christianity. Therefore, that is why a constant assault has been inflicted on Christianity, because it is the largest religion in the United States. If the influence of Christianity can be minimized here in the United States, then Judaism, Islam, Buddhism, Hinduism, and other forms of religion practiced here in the United States will fall much more easily. Most do not know it, but in the United States, Christianity is the big brother to all other religions. As long as Christians can protect their right to practice their religion as they see fit, then the other religions benefit from this as well, as it also protects their rights. What the media must understand is their assault on religion and morality will eventually cascade into their demise as well, just as we showed in the cascading nature of the First Amendment earlier. To avoid this, the press should and must look at itself as the protectors of truth and fact, and they must conduct themselves in a manner that reflects well on the high honor bestowed them. Many in the media will say that in a country that allows freedom of the press, they are not obligated to follow any such guidelines. We should be at a loss to understand how they can wrap themselves in a blanket of protection without honoring the device that provided them with the blanket in the first place. There also are no restrictions on what they report or say, provided it is truthful and factual, nor should there be, provided equal coverage and the same devotion are given to the other side of a debate or idea. The press should conduct themselves much like referees: they should be neutral to the outcome of such debates or ideas. Let the people decide with the facts provided by the media what the outcome should be.

Please, do not misinterpret these statements; this should only apply to reporting the news and events. It does not, and should not, have any bearing on editorials. It cannot be made clear enough, editorials and opinion can reflect any view at all, whether it is liberal, conservative, or moderate, without regard for any other viewpoint and without regard to any facts. Let us also not forget that if someone disagrees with a viewpoint, as I am sure many people will disagree with me, that is perfectly acceptable, and they too should be allowed an avenue to voice their dissent. Anyone who has the courage to voice their opinions, concerns, or ideas should be respected for their courage, even though you may disagree with everything they stand for. It is just as much an individual's right to think someone a fool and shun him or her or boycott him or her. Or—dare this word to be used— "censor them." That is right. Individuals have the right to censor other people. Publishers have the right to refuse publication. Record labels have the right to refuse recording. Radio stations have the right to refuse playing any song. All these outlets are privately owned, and along with that go the right of the individual and their opinions. It is true the word *censor* arouses fanaticism that will undoubtedly spur statements like "You can't censor anybody—that's against the law!" and "You should be put in jail!" To understand this properly, you must understand that if you own a television or radio, you have the right to censor what comes into your home, *because you own the television.* If, you choose not to watch a program, you are perfectly within your rights not to view it. However, the government does not have the right to tell you not to view it. You owning your television is no different from an individual owning a radio or television station. If he/she chooses not to allow something on their station, they are perfectly within their rights not to. If you disapprove, then your can listen or watch a station that will allow it. The word *censor* arouses ignorance. Censor (pronounced "senser") means to exercise control over something. Now that the definition is clear, how could anyone think that an individual does not have the right to exercise control over his/her own life or privately owned business? Again, only the government does not have the right to censorship, meaning the government cannot tell a newspaper what to print, or a radio station what to play; for that matter, they cannot tell a newspaper what *not* to print or a radio station what *not* to play, provided, of course, that it is not inflammatory and meets decency standards prescribed by the appropriate governing authority. The media relies on the limited knowledge of the average citizen and tries to exploit it to the fullest.

A perfect example is the story concerning the Dixie Chicks, the country girls' band that, while overseas, made disparaging remarks about President George Bush. For the record, they had the right to make any comments or statements they wanted. That being acknowledged, you must understand one individual's rights do not supersede another individual's rights. However, when radio stations quit playing their music and people quit buying their music, the media jumped with the headlines of "censorship." What you did not hear was that individuals and radio station owners were just exercising their right not to buy or play the Dixie Chicks' music. The media built it up as illegal activity. What is more disturbing is that some elected officials did too. What the citizens need to know and realize is that if someone does disagree with you, they still have rights too. They have just as much right not to listen to you as you do to speak. The media was trying to mislead by the omission of facts. They tried to make individuals think any censorship by anyone or any privately owned company was illegal. The media often uses this ploy of omission in reporting. If, in the editorial sections, there was some disagreement and an individual does not think this is right, then fine, but to try to pass it off, as headline news is completely a breach of trust and malpractice. My point is that all of the politicians and media that engaged in this knew that there was nothing illegal about what these radio stations did, yet they made continuous efforts to convince the American people otherwise. I realize I may come from "flyover country," but where I come from, we call that blatant lying. If that is not lying, then the only other explanation is that they are stupid and ignorant. It should be left to you, as the reader; to choose which category best defines them.

The media also likes to try to control conservative politicians by constantly using the words *partisan* and *bipartisan*. They keep printing stories about how America wants the political parties to get along and work together. Some politicians notice this and say, "We have to work in a spirit of bi-partisanship," and so on and so on. Well, to all the media outlets and individuals believing that garbage, it would be very interesting to see if, every time a candidate runs a commercial that says he/she will fight for the common man—that he/she will fight to get their ideas passed into law—the media would merely ask them, "If you are going to Congress to work in a bi-partisan manner, why would you have to fight with anyone? If you are going to get along with the other party, what is there to fight about?" Newspersons have all this college and formal education, so why hasn't some reporter or network news anchor thought to ask these questions? Why don't they ask those politicians about the ads they ran trying to get into the respective offices, illustrating the candidate as a champion of ideas that will challenge the opposition and fight for the common person? Because, they do not want to ask a question that will debunk what they have been perpetuating as news. Again, they constantly report gridlock as if it was a bad thing, and many times, this is not the case. One should be willing to demonstrate compromise on the "non-values and operational" debates. What one should not demonstrate compromise on are one's "values and morals" debates. Nor should one want the people one voted for to compromise on them. You as a citizen should stand strong for that in which you believe, regardless of whether you are liberal or conservative. You have the right to vote for whomever you choose, and you have the right to expect your candidate to fight for you and your ideals, no matter who disagrees with you. The media plays the "you are stupid and we are smart" card. They view themselves as the outlet for answers, the almighty oracle. In many cases, they know less than you do. They will at times purposely mislead their own listeners or readers. I have always thought that if I had a friend that asked me a question, I owed it to him/her to tell him/her the truth, regardless of how upset with me they may become, regardless of whether or not they would ever speak to me again. How nice it would be if a media outlet thought that way. The big difference is that I do not advertise other people's products to my friends for money, so I have no financial stake if they never talk to me again. The media, however, has a financial stake involved: if their customers get mad at them, they could lose money.

The *New York Times* sells 1.1 million newspapers a day at $1.75 each. Quite a stake indeed, if the public stops buying their paper. The three largest media markets in the United States are New York, Los Angeles, and Chicago—all Democrat strongholds. What do you think sells better in Indianapolis, an Indianapolis Colts jersey or a Tampa Bay Buccaneers jersey? Why do you think that is? The answer is, most assuredly, there are more Colts fans in Indianapolis than Tampa Bay fans. Therefore, it is best to sell a product that is more tailored to the community in question. Even Democrats will tell you that New York City, Los Angeles, and Chicago are predominantly Democrat. It is not hard to see that in a particular market, the news may want to sugarcoat the criticism or blow it out of proportion, depending on political leanings. This type of behavior has tarnished the media as a whole. They have actually been a party to aiding and abetting liars. There have been many candidates that lie, and the media knows they are lying, and they do not call them on it. I am a conservative, and I vote conservative. However, if I think or know that a conservative is lying, I want them caught. You see, I am not foolish enough to think all conservatives tell the truth and all liberals lie. If a conservative can admit that, why can't a liberal admit that? However, there are people on both sides that will not admit that some candidates with their respective affiliation lie. The people bring some of this on themselves by not wanting to recognize the cold, hard truth as just that. If it goes against what they have always been told, then it must be wrong. It makes no difference how many facts one might present; they simply refuse to acknowledge them as truth. They prefer manufactured evidence as long as it coincides with their personal beliefs. To say otherwise, you must be a heretic. Just ask Copernicus. Is it any wonder the media is reluctant to report all the facts? It should not be regarding the financial aspect; however, since the media has a duty in a free society to report the truth, it should be. Some time ago, the media was constantly reporting on Rep. Tom Delay (R) for possible wrongdoing with contributions. It was on the television, radio, and newspapers every day. Rep. William Jefferson (D) was found to have $75,000 in his freezer; there was not and there still has not been an outcry from the media. Whether either one of these men is guilty or innocent is unknown; however, what is good for the goose is good for the gander. The fact is, when the Justice Department wanted to search Rep. William Jefferson's congressional office, Congress, with help from both sides of the aisle, Republican and Democrat alike, tried to say this was violating the sanctity of Congress. Imagine that—some politicians actually saying they should have a place that is off-limits to a legal search and seizure. That is an indicator right there that some think they are above the law. That was on both sides of the political aisle, mind you. They tried to obstruct a properly executed search warrant signed by a judge. Apparently, they think they are above the U.S. Constitution as well. This is why people are growing frustrated with the system. What they need to realize is the system is fine; it is some of the people in the system that are wrong. I reiterate; you will find these people on both political sides. It is the role of the media to tell us which ones these are. They had the information on those trying to obstruct the search; why not publicize it to everyone?

Another way the media tries to manufacture credibility is by putting celebrity faces on their cause. When a celebrity speaks, the media acts as if the individual has a degree or professional experience regarding the subject matter. In most cases, this could not be further from the truth. Most movie stars, singing stars, or performers that have reached celebrity status never went to college, let alone have a degree. Nor do most have any professional expertise concerning the topic of what they are speaking. So where does their expertise come from? Exactly— more times than not, they really do not have a clue about what they are talking about. They have done no practical research themselves; they are merely relying on what someone else has told them—someone that is steering an agenda. Do not get me wrong; celebrities, like everyone else, are certainly entitled to their opinion. However, it probably should not be given any more credibility than that of your local mechanic, carpenter, or any other average person speaking about something outside their area of expertise. Do not misunderstand; many celebrities have lent their names, reputations, and more to very good causes. Danny Thomas and Jerry Lewis immediately come to mind, but it seems that when celebrities venture out and involve themselves in quasi-political issues, they in most cases are vastly ill-informed and do not have an educated point of view. They tend to choose the more popular direction, which in turn makes them more popular, but not necessarily correct.

If the newspapers actually wanted people to know the truth about politics and politicians, they would have a section of the paper devoted to the votes before the House and Senate. "Silly," you say, "they print sports sections, life sections, entertainment sections, and employment sections. Every time we get into an election cycle, the news networks have time devoted to the upcoming political election." As with sports, they could have "box scores": we could know how people voted, who voted yea, who voted nay, who abstained, who was not present and why. This way, people could track their local representatives and senators to find out how each one voted; then we would not have to wonder if our elected officials are actually doing what we sent them there to do. The newspapers would claim they already do report this via the front page, but unfortunately, what we do not see there is what is voted on and the actual breakdowns of how everyone voted. Most people do not know what their representative does every day or how he/she votes. If it was their favorite sports team, they could tell who was dogging it and who was giving it their all. The fans would want the player who was dogging it traded or released. What a novel idea for politicians, if more and more citizens started giving them walking papers based on their day-to-day performance. If more citizens were aware of what went on in our capital, then more citizens would know when a particular representative or senator was doing or saying something ridiculous. This would be an exciting way for the news media to reclaim the role, which was granted them by the First Amendment, and not simply spew their own opinions as news.

The only other question is whether or not there is a market for it. There are many people who vote in all the elections; perhaps those people would be interested in obtaining facts before casting their ballots.

Disgruntlement #2:
CONGRESS AND OUR MONEY

There is hardly a day that goes by that my children do not spend my money. They naturally have necessities that are my responsibility to pay for. To make enough money to cover paying for the medical insurance, dental insurance, deductibles, groceries, school supplies, clothing, and entertainment—as well as a multitude of expenses that don't immediately come to mind—requires one to work extremely long hours. I leave for work about 6:00 a.m. every morning. Sometimes when I come home around

5:00 p.m., I bring my work home with me and work on it until the wee hours of the morning. I dearly love my children, and I have no problem fulfilling my responsibilities. However, constant frustration is caused by what seems to be a misappropriation of the family funds. You know—the lights that are left on with no one in the room, trips back to the store for something for school when you were only there a few minutes ago, having them make plans for you to supply transportation for their friends to come over as well as pay for the pizza when they get there, not to mention all the things they break or lose that have to be replaced. It is very demoralizing, and it has been known to make me very angry. It is absolutely amazing, the ease with which they just keep coming back to the money well and expect the bucket to always be full. They truly remind me of our United States Congress. The audacity that representatives and senators have is unbelievable. Both the Senate and the House of Representatives propose a budget every year of how to spend the citizens of this country's money. They definitely have important necessities to pay for, which is understandable. However, the pork-laden bills they propose, where basically, they skim from the top money that does not belong to them, that truly belongs to the people of the United States, for their pet projects in their respective areas of representation, all for the express purpose of getting them re-elected—that does create a problem. This should make us all angry; many times, the American people are. Many representatives and senators try to pretend they are looking out for your money, and if the president is a Republican, then the Democrats blame the president. If the president is a Democrat, the Republicans blame the president. They will blame each other as well, but none will take on the responsibility for their own actions. They rely on the ignorance of the majority of Americans concerning the Constitution. For instance, the duties defined by the U.S. Constitution, Article 1, Section 7: "All bills for raising revenue shall originate in the House of Representatives; but the Senate may propose or concur with amendments as on other Bills." In other words, all taxes and levies and spending cannot happen without majority consent from the entire Congress. There are 435 representatives in the House and 100 senators in the Senate. So before a president can sign any budget or any law or veto the same, at least 218 representatives and at least 50 senators (with the vice president's vote in case of a tie) must agree with the legislation. If it is a bad budget, a total of no less than 270 people in government are just as guilty of its passage—not just the president, as many would have you believe. Congress has more to do with how our money is spent than the president. Congress is responsible for how much tax we are levied, Congress, and Congress alone is responsible for spending the money via the budget. The money the government spends on procurement is so far unbalanced it is utterly ridiculous. For the last fifteen years, I have made my living selling building materials to commercial and residential contractors, as well as having several relatives in the construction business. Trust me when I say, "Congress will authorize sometimes as much as ten times more than a project should cost to be completed." Why? It is easy to spend "other people's" money. (Keep in mind; the "other people" to whom I am referring are you, the American taxpayer.) Like my children, the politicians think the money well is always full. If they really cared about the common person as they claim, they would find a way to make government services cost less. Instead, project costs are padded in order to gain political influence. They either know this and do not care or do not know this and are too incompetent to hold office. Either way, it does not reflect well on our Congress. Many times, in the federal government, we have two or three people doing the same job or two or three documents to fill out that are asking for the same information repeatedly. The government procurement office is paying too much for services. When there is not enough money to cover the expenses, they merely raise our taxes. Think of it—they spend money that does not belong to them, for pet projects, and when there is a shortfall, they vote to take more money from us, the taxpayers. What would your employer think if you spent the employer's money to finance your pet project and when there was not enough, you simply went back to the cash drawer and took some more out? Your employer would not only fire you, but also have you arrested for theft. Unfortunately, for us, Congress is fleecing the citizens legally by virtue of the Constitution, which has empowered them; do not blame the Constitution, just the employers of Congress for not paying attention. (If you need reminding again, we are the employers.) The Constitution that empowers Congress is the same one that empowers us as citizens. We do have an option, as your employer does: we can terminate their employment.

How do different sections and entities of the government drain the budget? Take, for example, a government department that was given fifty million dollars for the 2007 fiscal year. In the last quarter of the fiscal year, if that department is under budget, it starts to spend money needlessly in order to ensure that it maximizes its budget allocation. The department will do this in an effort to ensure that it does not have its 2008 fiscal year budget cut back to how much it would have spent in the 2007 fiscal year. Every department that operates under budget does this. The sad part is, Congress knows this as well, every last one of them, Republican, Democrat, an independent alike. Do you hear that noise? It sounds like someone gasping for air. That is the sound of every politician who feels like they were just punched in the stomach. What we should have been hearing, for a long time now, are some of our elected officials standing on the rooftops crying, "Foul!" The federal government needs to learn how to balance the budget and restrain themselves from shopping sprees with the people's money. Consider every office or department in the government using this practice. The politicians have stood by and allowed it. Perhaps some have even participated in it. The media did break a story years ago about the three-hundred-dollar hammer and seven-hundred-dollar toilet seat; however, after a cool-down period, the government is right back at it.

The rank and file U.S Representatives and U.S. Senators make $162,500–per-year salary from the government. That is $85,937,500 in salaries per year. Are we getting our money's worth, or do we need more bang for the buck? Let us not forget, there are *not*_many persons in our Congress that were poor to start with. This should not be turned into class warfare; however, it should be noted for the people out there that live paycheck to paycheck. There are times when they actually write a check two days before payday to buy groceries for their families. We need our money to be well spent. We do not mind paying taxes, but please do not waste our hard-earned money. Everywhere you look, you find government waste. Congress has a duty to protect the American people from this kind of abuse. The media has a duty to expose it as well.

Have you ever noticed that when the government votes on a bill, it has some ridiculous amount of pages, like 1,342 pages or some other crazy number? Have you ever wondered if your representative read what they are voting for or if they just read a couple of pages from the part in which they were interested? That is how the committees sneak in pay raises or the aforementioned pork-laden projects. When a person of Congress wants to seem like they care about you, they often propose new programs to assist you. They raise taxes on you to pay for the program, and take even more of your money. Perhaps if they maintained the U.S. budget, as we are required to maintain our budgets at home, they could give us our money back and we would not need another program. The current programs in place are usually a debacle when you take a close look at them. Even when the government tries to help, somehow the people get the shaft. Residing in Picayune, Mississippi, I was here during Hurricane Katrina. The federal government assisted with what has become well known as the FEMA Trailer. Thankfully, I never needed one. The people should be aware that our government paid as much as $75,000 per trailer, in total cost, from manufacturing, delivery, and set-up. The federal government purchased trailers that were worth about $5,000 for who knows how much and paid out a ridiculous fee to different companies to arrange delivery and set-up. According to the most accounts, there are over 90,000 FEMA trailers occupied in Mississippi and approximately 30,000 occupied in the greater New Orleans metro area, an approximate total of 120,000 at $75,000 each, for the sum of $9,000,000,000. You have probably seen the damage from previous hurricanes in Florida, Alabama, Mississippi, and Louisiana; do you recall seeing the blue tarp roofs? Each one of those roofs cost approximately $2,000. My roof lost shingles as well, and the next day after Katrina, I purchased a blue tarp from my employer and covered my roof. The tarp and the simplex nails to put it down with cost about $50. Not only did they spend far too much money on these projects, but they also inflated the labor market for the area with these outrageous contracts with the contractors to set up the FEMA trailers and tarp people's roofs. My son, now seventeen years old, with no experience, was being paid a general labor rate of over $15.00 per hour doing remodeling. How much do you think an experienced person was getting? When I built my house, roofing labor was $23.00 per 100 square feet; after Katrina, it was over $100.00 per 100 square feet. It was not greed by the roofing contractors; they had to pay labor the same amount the FEMA contractors were paying the labor or lose their people. The labor market was so inflated that it not only affected the construction market but other markets as well. The housing industry, with an incredible demand for homes at that time, found it difficult to get homes built because the labor was too high for appraisal values. The labor market is cooling down now, which has caused a glut of inventory for houses that were built after Katrina, because they are more expensive than what the market will bear. This is a direct result of the overspending of our government. This will have further impact on residents in the Louisiana and Mississippi area, as the labor rates are still too high for them to rebuild with the money from insurance disbursements and other government programs and funds.

Another way Congress wastes our money is for political gain, to either take credit for creating another well intentioned but poorly thought out program or has congressional hearings on matters that are already covered by the law and the Constitution. They do this by pretending law and the Constitution do not cover the matters. Currently, we are witness to just one of these hearings. President Bush, like his predecessor, President Clinton, has dismissed some federal prosecutors. Senators Charles Schumer, Ted Kennedy, and Hillary Clinton have taken exception to this. They know the President of the United States is perfectly within the rights of the office to dismiss a federal appointee for any reason. (Supreme Court Justices are an exception.) It does not even have to be a good reason. President Clinton dismissed ninety-three federal prosecutors, while President Bush fired eight. For the mathematically impaired, that is 8.6% of the number that President Clinton fired. Senator Schumer and his cohorts are spending in their salary alone $8,500 per day, not to mention the salaries of their staff, to hold these hearings all to find out if President Bush dismissed these prosecutors without just cause. Even if they find this to be true, it does not matter, because he did not need just cause—no more than President Clinton needed just cause when he dismissed ninety-three. Once again, the media knows this, but chooses not to drop the story; if they did drop the story, you would see the hearings wrap up at an incredible rate. Senator Charles Schumer (D-New York), along with Senator Ted Kennedy (D–Massachusetts), would rather spend the taxpayers' money seeking to milk political points from their base and at the same time hopefully convince some people who are not aware that any president is within his province to dismiss any federal appointee that some law was broken and some scandal is in the works. In Senator Schumer's defense, he was not serving as a senator when President Clinton dismissed the ninety-three federal prosecutors, so we do not know whether he would have had the same reaction then as now. However, the double speaking senator from Massachusetts, Senator Ted Kennedy (D) was, and he defended the dismissals under President Clinton. Senator Hillary Clinton did not take exception with her husband for his firings. Why do they have a problem with it now? In addition, once again, why hasn't the news media pointed this very fact out to the American public? Earlier it was stated that on morals and values, congressional representatives should fight for what they believe in. However, this fighting for political gain, while spending the taxpayers' money too, must stop.

Alexander Hamilton once said, "Men often oppose a thing merely because they had no agency in planning it, or because it may have been planned by those whom they dislike." He could not have been more right than today. Too many times, we have seen legislation blocked by both parties to keep the one party from getting credit for a good law. If it is good for America, why should it matter who gets credit? It probably would not under normal circumstances if it weren't for political power and political gain, all the while spending more and more money having hearings, votes, and re-votes to pass legislation. One day perhaps in the not-so-distant future will rise a leader from the political rabble, someone who will tell it like it is regardless of what political group he/ she offends or defends. Someone that will put the citizenry of the United States first and foremost, over politics and over money and over power. When this happens, perhaps enough people will have tired of the status quo in politics and stand behind this leader.

Hopefully, when a leader does come about, we can tackle the educational shortfalls we have been demonstrating for some time now. This is one more major area where Congress spends too much money. If you consider how much money is spent on public education, there is no reason teachers should not be well paid and students should not receive a fantastic education. According to School Matters, a service of the Standard and Poors, the total funding for elementary and secondary education for the 2004-05 school year was $536,000,000,000. According to that same report, there were 49,370,553 students in public school in 2005, with the total expenditures (federal, state and local) at $9,414 per student. According to the CATO Institute, the cost of tuition at the average private school $3,116 per student. The only thing missing from private schools that public schools have is transportation. If you can safely put sixty children on a school bus, considering you have a difference of $6,298 per child, you would have to spend $377,880 per year on a bus for a salaried bus driver, diesel fuel, and maintenance, to make up the difference of the cost per child. If you spent $1,000 per week on fuel and paid a bus driver $40,000 per year (fantastic pay for a part-time job) that is only $76,000. If you add in another $15,000 for maintenance per bus, that brings the total transportation to about $91,000 per busload of sixty children. The difference in education would now be $4,781.33 per child. If you multiply that by 49,370,553 (the number of public school students in 2005 the U.S). You have a total savings of $236,056,906,175.49. Actually, the savings would be much higher, because these figures consider that everyone would ride the bus. Many high-school-aged children drive to school, many children walk to school, and many children have their parents drive them to school. Therefore, you would have to add the cost difference of $1,516.67 back to the savings for every child that has an alternate method of transportation to school. Without having an exact number on how many children get to school by other methods than riding the bus, that extra savings is difficult to pinpoint. The government could create vouchers to be used for private schools, allowing the parents to choose what school their children attended. A cost-of-living allowance could be put in place that would allow consideration for particular areas. They government could provide transportation in the form of school buses, as we have already allotted $91,000 a year per bus before we considered our savings. Those that say a bus costs more to purchase than that amount need only to be reminded we already have many buses for public school in existence for which the government is already paying, not to mention it would not be necessary to replace every bus every year.

Three strong reasons for school vouchers for everyone:

1. Many detractors, like the teachers' union, would say that too many teachers and educators would lose their jobs. Nothing could be further from

the truth. When more private schools opened, there would be competition for students, and there would be competition for teachers as well. How do institutions compete for teachers? With more money and better benefits, that is how. The only teachers that would be in danger would be the sub-par teachers. This would require them to become better in order to make a living.

2. The sub-par students would become better because they would have better teachers. Also, keep in mind that most parents want the best for their children. Many in Congress send their children to private schools. We should follow their lead; in doing so, we could save a lot of tax money. Your children could be better prepared for college, and even if college weren't for them, they would have a better, well-rounded education. Suddenly, the children of the middle class and poorer neighborhoods would be able to compete academically with the children of the more financially secure.

3. This would not only fix the educational deficit with the other industrialized nations, but would also fix the educational deficit between races and neighborhoods. We could better our education facilities, our curriculum, and our children's opportunities while saving billions in taxpayer money if Congress wants to fix the problem—or perhaps they will try to discredit it in some way so they can keep education spiraling downward into

a black hole, all the while risking the futures of *your children*, not *their children.* Every company or corporation will tell you their most valuable asset is the human resources. That stands true for this country as well; our children are our most valuable asset as well as this country's. We must make every effort to ensure that our children receive the best possible education the world has to offer.

Are we now experiencing what the early settlers of this nation called "taxation without representation"? We have representatives and senators, but are they truly representing the American people, or are they representing themselves? Both political parties seem more concerned with keeping themselves in power than with really establishing a positive change in this country. The hard-working people of this nation, both Democrat and Republican, are growing tired of being taken for granted and being taken advantage of. No one should expect either political party to give up on their values. That being said, both parties should be working much harder trying to keep our hard-earned money in our pockets. If they cared more about the American people, then doing the right thing would be easy, even if it meant they might not be re-elected. They would be willing to let themselves be judged by their deeds, not their words. They cannot see the trees for the forest; re-election would take care of itself if they demonstrated that their primary concern was for the people. All the figures that have been cited in this chapter are available to the public on the internet. Do not take my word for it—investigate it yourself. The trust is appreciated that some readers may have in these figures; however, remember the words of President Ronald Reagan: "...trust, but verify...."

Disgruntlement #3:
POLITICAL CORRECTNESS AND HISTORY

Political correctness is defined as a means of making the truth digestible to a particular segment of the populace—in other words, "flavoring the medicine." It sounds benign, unless the flavoring diminishes or counteracts the medicine itself. If the medicine can heal us more effectively and faster without the flavor, just give it to us straight. Even if it tastes bad, even if we do not like it, we still want the real stuff.

Political correctness is one way in which the beacon of ignorance is at its brightest.

Every human being should be afforded the utmost dignity and respect. Certain names and phrases should be discarded, not in the name of political correctness, but in the name of decency. Ignorance and stupidity are fertile fields for intolerance and bigotry, hate and rage. Many a dictator has sown and harvested these fruits for his own personal gain. This is another reason for truth and fact. The very term *political correctness* lends itself to deceit. If *correct* means true or right, then preceding the word *correct* with *political* or any other adjective infers something other than true or right. History is a wonderful tool and guide for us to study. However, that does not mean that all history is wonderful and pretty. In fact, a lot of history is quite disgusting and ugly. We need to learn from the palatable and non-palatable history. Although I believe that history can be divided into different periods, it is silly to think history can be divided into different races or religions. To do so would suggest that there is no intertwining of races or religions. In other words, in the history of Christianity, you had the Inquisition and the Crusades. These events were against other religions, the Jews and Moslems. So for all three of these religions, these events happened. There may be different viewpoints of cause and result, but the events in question had only one occurrence. Let us take, for example, five people witnessing something, like a car accident. There may be different views and versions of what happened; some may be right, perhaps none.

However, there was only one accident. Someone's viewpoint or account does not actually change what happened. The only way we have to determine what did happen is too truthfully and factually record it. As our means of recording history improves via audio and visual aids, then the more accurate, the seeing of history will become. However, one must still be concerned about the narration of history. Many rationalize the use of political correctness in history so as not to offend someone. However, why would someone be offended by the truth? It may be shameful or embarrassing, but the truth is the truth. One cannot make decisions as to one's future unless one knows the real truth, not the politically correct truth. So when you hear "politically correct," listen with skepticism. Many of our political leaders hide behind these words, and the media, again, is quick to attack if they can make someone seem like a racist or religious zealot—even if the one being attacked may be telling the truth. There have been many injustices in the history of man; some of them have had horrendous impacts on humanity. It is those who do not have a complete understanding of history that will refuse to believe that all events throughout the world affect everyone all over the world eventually. Even the history that is ugly and disgusting can be learned from, but only if you are not afraid to face it. Because the human race is a constantly changing group, even negative occurrences can grow to have a positive impact on the people that come afterward. For instance, most people would agree that illness and disease are not good things, and no one wants to see anyone sick. However, in about the mid-1950s, my grandfather and great-uncle were both ill. They would both be in and out of the hospital, until one day, they were in the same room at the same time. They did not know each other until that day. How is this possible? Well, it is not hard to explain at all. My father went to visit his father (my grandfather), and my mother went to visit her uncle (my great-uncle), and that is where my parents met for the first time. One might say that is where my history started. They would be wrong, of course; my history started long before, throughout time long before I was born. It took different twist until it arrived to me, and it will take different twist before it arrives to my descendants. What if my grandfather and great-uncle had never been ill? Their misfortunate illness was a major reason I exist. That does not make it good, but it is the truth.

History is wrought with sadness, pain, and unfairness. They are many things in this world that sadden us and that we dislike. We may not like the fact that Abraham Lincoln and Martin Luther King Jr. were assassinated. Just because we do not like it does not change the fact that they were assassinated. History has nothing to do with likes and dislikes. John Wilkes Booth and James Earl Ray were the individuals that were guilty of the crimes, which were a result of hatred, rage, ignorance, and stupidity. (All of these things should sadden us, and we should dislike them.)

It is human nature that no one likes to be thought of as ignorant or stupid—not even ignorant or stupid people. That being acknowledged, for those people that are ignorant or stupid that are *not* naturally smarter or wiser than anyone else is, they must manufacture in their minds someone that is more ignorant and stupid than they are. This is why racism and bigotry are such tough opponents. If you doubt this, ask yourself, "If there were no ignorant or stupid people in the world today, what would happen to racism and bigotry? What would happen to political correctness?" There would be no need for it. Why? Because smart and wise people can handle the truth and dissect it properly without malice to anyone else. This indicates that either political correctness is specifically made for stupid and ignorant people or for people the *media* thinks of as stupid or ignorant.

Political correctness has no place in history. Imagine yourself sitting in a jury box, trying to decipher the truth of right or wrong, and the attorneys and judge involved could not tell the whole truth because someone might be offended. How would you ever come to a good verdict? When my children involve themselves in a situation, I ask them to tell me the truth. I may then hear something that saddens and disappoints or even angers me. I prefer that to being lied to, and I prefer the truth to having important aspects to the story omitted—which, by the way, is the same as outright lying anyway. I want to know exactly what happened. Once all the facts are in order, a determination of right and wrong will be made without the assistance of outside opinion. Many times, the media tries to rationalize actions or positions as they are reporting them. They should leave that to the people. Truthfully, political correctness is like talking to one's spouse and trying to be careful not to anger him/her. It is like trying to discuss an issue while dancing around the issue. The only problem is that you rarely, if ever, resolve your issue, and it invariably arises in the future. Perhaps it is being naïve, but if something is wrong, it is wrong; it needs no adjectives to enhance the meaning. If something is correct, it is correct; it also needs no adjectives to enhance the meaning. We have to learn to communicate with each other without all the fear of reprisal. There will always be people out there that are ignorant and refuse to accept truth, but that does not mean we have to accommodate them. We must build a coalition of all people of all races and religions and of both sexes that demand the truth, regardless of any embarrassment it may cause to a particular group. This will be difficult with the current media habits as they are, when they have done much to perpetuate ignorance. It must be stressed that there will be pain and embarrassment for all, because no one group of people are without fault and no one group of people is perfect. However, the truth will help everyone understand our plight as a nation. We must learn from the past so we can build for the future.

Political correctness is a way that the media can whitewash the truth while at the same time making minorities feel that they are looking out for their best interest and what is right. Even if it skews the truth or leaves out pertinent details to the truth, they do this to make themselves look fair and understanding and above divisive issues. It is another avenue of many for politicians to speak to us as if we are morons, with the attitude that only they themselves can enlighten us. Yet, these are problems that can only be repaired by the nation as a whole. All parties must come to the realization that we are a mightier nation when we stand together. When we realize this truth and have empathy for our fellow neighbor, when we consider and respect the trials and tribulations of others, we can be an even stronger nation indeed. When we seek to rationalize our actions of today by the actions of others in the past, we must keep in mind that we may not be able to climb back up that slippery slope.

Rationalize is defined by the Encarta Dictionary as an attempt to justify behavior normally considered irrational or unacceptable by offering an apparently reasonable explanation. That is a very dangerous definition, don't you think? We could all rationalize every decision we ever made.

Justify is defined by the Encarta Dictionary as to serve as an acceptable reason or excuse for something.

One means the attempt to give good reason, and one means with good reason.

So, what is the big difference? Let us take the three-fifths compromise for example.

This was a compromise between the northern and southern states, reached during the Constitutional Convention of 1787. The southern states, in an effort to gain political power, wanted slaves to be counted in the census; this would affect the appointment of delegates and representatives. This was extremely important because at that time, according to census of 1790, which would occur three years later, the slaves in the South consisted of almost 700,000 people. The entire population of the country was just under four million; approximately 17.5% of the entire population of the country was slaves. This would dramatically affect the House of Representatives. The House of Representatives would elect the president of the United States. The northern states wanted no part of this. The northern states knew this would tip the balance of power to the South. For the most part, it was not because the North was so concerned with the welfare of an enslaved people, although some, like the second president, John Adams, were adamantly opposed to slavery. However, for most people, make no mistake about it, it was about political power. The North's contention was that slaves could not vote, and they did not want them counted at all. After all, why should slaves be counted as a means of determining how many representatives a state would have if slaves were not going to be represented? The answer to the compromise came down to money. Yes, as usual, follow the money trail. The North proposed that if slaves were counted in the census, they should be taxed accordingly. In other words, the South would have to purchase the representation. There was haggling over this issue. After the two-thirds proposal and the three-quarters proposal could not gain support, each side relented and accepted the three-fifths proposal, and it became law. The population of slaves and indentured servants would be counted and multiplied by sixty percent. The Constitution does not and never has directly stated that each slave or indentured servant was only sixty percent of a man or woman. However, it essentially did. One could rationalize that if the southern states had been able to count 100% of the enslaved population, slavery might have gone on even longer, because Abraham Lincoln would not have been elected. Could they actually justify it, though? There is a lot of history entwined in this constitutional compromise. The Missouri Compromise for example, which limited the number of slave states, would not have happened, because there would not have been a need to compromise; the southern states would have had enough votes without it. However, no one should think for one moment that if the South had been able to count the enslaved population as 100%, that meant they would have afforded slaves the rights of every other citizen. The fact is, the Supreme Court under the Dred Scott decision said that slaves or the descendants of slaves could not be citizens and therefore were afforded no rights under the Constitution. (The majority of the Supreme Court at that time was made up of Democrats from slave states.) In addition, how, is it possible to consider a group of the population as three-fifths of the whole, yet consider the individuals of that same group 100% of a person? How would have history been affected if even more Supreme Court justices had been from the southern states at that time? Do the events in relation to a time period have any bearing on right or wrong? Whether by design or coincidence, did events unfold in the only sequence possible to gradually free a people? These are questions that are good for discussion for all men and women; it allows us to have a better understanding of one another and educates us as well, so we do not make the same mistakes our ancestors made. I do not know the answers to all these questions; there is no way to know, as history does not get a second chance. I do know that whatever the answers may be, we follow a dangerous path if we allow the ends to justify the means. Once something is done, it is done. You cannot replay it and alter events to get the desired effect. It does allow us to carefully consider our actions and beliefs now. Each and every one of us makes history every day. How do we conduct ourselves with all people? We cannot control the actions of others, only our own. We all should seek to learn from one another, as well as learn on our own, how history unfolded and discuss it openly, without reservation. We will not conquer the ills of racism and bigotry overnight. We can, however, pave the road to a future that allows each of us to respect those that are similar to us as ourselves, as well those that are different from us.

One way to do this is to not be tainted by the media and their political correctness. So many people are afraid of being considered bigots or chauvinists that they are afraid to speak correctly. Even the politicians are afraid of being labeled by the media. For instance, in the House of Representatives and the Senate, when a representative or senator refers to a member as the gentleman from a particular state or the gentle lady from a particular state. Okay, I know another definition from my friends from Encarta Dictionary. (Lady: a woman who behaves very politely and with dignity. Gentleman: a cultured man who behaves with courtesy and thoughtfulness.) To refer to a lady as a gentle lady in a political regard is to be redundant. It is like saying "the gentle gentleman" or starting an event by saying, "Gentle ladies and gentlemen." It sounds rather crass, and it truly shows the utmost ignorance of people and the fear of reprisal of women's groups. All done because of political correctness. When does it end? Where does it end? As a single father of four boys, when my twins were in diapers, time was not spent complaining to the advocacy groups that the WIC center (Women with Infant Children) was not called the PIC center (Parents with Infant Children). It is utterly ridiculous when we overlook the good that organization does for all people and focus on the politically correct name of the organization. We are in danger when normally intelligent people acquiesce to the demands of the ignorant because it is easier than trying to educate them. We see it every day, all around us. We grow outraged at silliness and let the obvious pass by undetected, all because many of the elected officials and media outlets are trying to look like they are fair and just instead of *being* fair and just. For instance, would they ever ponder why, if someone was looking for Mrs. Smith in an office, and she is the only woman in that office, and she happens to be pregnant, many people would say, "Go into the office and look for the pregnant woman" instead of "Look for the woman"? Why do you need to describe her as pregnant? If Mr. Jones is the only man in the office and happens to be black, why do so many say, "Look for the black man" instead of "Look for the man"? I personally believe there is not necessarily any animus intended, but perhaps we all could learn from this example. Perhaps the politicians and the media could too.

Many will state that they want to change history or they want to change the future. It could be argued that one can no more change tomorrow than change yesterday. That argument will be made here. Yesterday is gone, and tomorrow never comes. However, we are here today in the present with the power to conduct ourselves in a positive way. If we start working on the "todays," then the tomorrows will unfold into the yesterdays, and history may have less pain and sadness. The future will begin to look brighter for everyone.

Disgruntlement #4:
TODAY'S YOUTH

For the most part, an abundant number of today's youth have possibly been damaged beyond repair. They have been damaged due to neglect—neglect from parents and schools. The liberal view of emancipating the young by allowing them adult privileges well before their time has proved to be the demise of many young men and women. Treating children as if they are grown and able to determine what is best for them is madness. How do I mean that, you ask? For quite some time now, the liberals, with help from the media, have become apologists for unacceptable behavior and all but banished corporal punishment from our society. Many Americans have tried to accelerate the maturity of children by allowing them to have privileges they are not yet ready for. In doing so, they have helped unleash a group of Americans that have minimal-to-no guidance and minimal-to-no discipline, as well as none of life's experiences to anchor any values whatsoever. Since the assault on corporal punishment, we as a nation have watched the high school dropout rate, teen pregnancy, teen abortion, teen crime, teen drug abuse, and teen alcoholism rise. If you were to go back and track the steady increase of this laundry list, you would see that it coincides with the decline of discipline in the home and in school. All the while the liberals and the media were crying," Let the children express themselves! Let them find out who they are." My mother made me who I am today, and *I thank her for it*. I will agree that my mother was much, more strict than I am today. Growing up, in my day, it was commonplace to see Mom dealing with her children in public. There was no reason to wait until we got home. We lived in a small town early in my youth, and when my mother went shopping, sometimes the aisle would be crowded. If, she said, "Children, stay by the cart while I go over on the other aisle," we had better be no more than an arm's length away from the cart when she got back. If not, we got our butts "tore up." She carried a switch, and she would spank us all the way back to that cart. I knew my mother was serious. I dared not defy her, nor talk back. At forty-five now, I still know it. That may seem rather stern to some of you. However, it taught to me and every one of my siblings that we were to behave properly in public—and private, for that matter. Why didn't anyone report her, you ask. Simple—they were too busy doing the same thing to their children as well. What was the result? It created a more disciplined and decent society. The truth is, civilizations from all over the world had been spanking their children for thousands of years; then suddenly the liberals decided that was the wrong way to raise your children, and in less than thirty years, we have many of the woes we have today. My mother's discipline did not stop in the home, either, if we misbehaved in school, she did not go to the school and complain to them that we were innocent. No, she reinforced their rules, and she reinforced them well. That is right—we got it twice. It was not long before we learned to keep our mouths shut, hoped, and prayed that my mother did not run into any of our teachers at the supermarket or somewhere else. Today, you see teenagers hanging out at the convenience store or on the corner somewhere. Have you ever been too frightened to stop and get gas or something else because the convenience store was the local hangout of thugs and punks? Not in my day. The parents would have stopped that long before it began, when the thugs and punks were young children. If my mother had given us a time to be home and we were not, "Lord help us." She would come looking for us, and when she found us, she would spank us all the way home. Some of you are probably thinking, "That was wrong. That was child abuse." The bleeding hearts will say that a child should never be embarrassed in public. They should consider, humility is an integral part of discipline. The next day at school, we could not lie and say "My mother did not care" or "My mother did not do anything." There were too many witnesses to the contrary. It is hard to grow up into a thug or punk when everyone knows your mother will put the smack down on you. To this day, we do not go around and use inappropriate language in public. We open doors for women, treating everyone with respect, especially our elders. We do not behave rudely towards anyone.

I walked to school every day, and if I misbehaved in school, I might have to erase and clean the chalkboard, as well as clean the erasers. This dramatically interfered with my fifteen-minute window I was allowed to walk home. I was not allowed to stop off anywhere; I had to come straight home. If my walk home took more than fifteen minutes from the time school let out, I had some explaining to do. Since I could not say I stopped somewhere, I usually thought of and rehearsed a lie until I was home. My mother then took no time at all figuring out I was lying, and I was in big trouble. I had got myself into double trouble—first for misbehaving in school, then for trying to deceive my mother. I was disciplined accordingly, the next day, I was more than happy to behave in school.

When I was in second grade, I walked with my older brothers in the fifth and sixth grades to the movies, over a mile down the highway into town almost every Sunday. We paid for our tickets out of the money we got selling newspapers on Wednesday for ten cents. We would walk about a mile to the newspaper office with our fifty-cent allowance, buy ten newspapers for a nickel apiece, and sell them for their face value of a dime. When Sunday came around, we each had one dollar to go to the movies with. It was fifty cents to get in, fifteen cents for popcorn, fifteen cents for a soda, and fifteen cents for a candy bar. My brothers and I still had a whole nickel for candy on the way home. My point is, we walked all over town and were never concerned about weirdoes or crazy people. Literally miles per week and not one incident. Quite the contrary, actually—most people were very nice and helpful. They were keeping an eye on us, all right. They actually helped keep us safe and out of trouble, as the community quietly helped with everyone's children. If we did do something wrong, someone in town would have taken us back to our parents. My parents would not have stood by the door arguing with the person about our innocence, either; we would have been dealt with.

Many people would say that times have changed since I was a child, and I would have to agree. However, let me interject again that times had changed from the 1700s to the 1970s, but what did not change was how people raised their children. What about the people that time span produced? People like George Washington, Thomas Jefferson, Alexander Hamilton, Abraham Lincoln, Theodore Roosevelt, Thomas Edison, George Washington Carver, Albert Einstein, Harry Truman, Ronald Reagan, Martin Luther King Jr. —the list goes on and on. That time span produced many good, hardworking, decent people from all groups of race, religion, and ethnicity. What was so wrong with that, I ask? Many of the woes that affect this nation can be traced back to the lack of basic discipline that children face at home and their regard for authority instilled in them at home by good ole' Mom and Dad. We cannot blame it entirely on Mom and Dad, because many of them fear retribution from law enforcement for disciplining their children. What strikes me as strange is that approximately eighty percent of the United States believes in corporal punishment. Yet, twenty percent of the malcontents that know more than anyone else have nothing better to do than stick their noses in other people's business. They feel that spanking is child abuse. Do not get me wrong—there are some sadistic and perverted people out there, and these people should be prosecuted to the fullest extent of the law. However, let us not throw the baby out with the bathwater. A good, old-fashioned "butt–whippin" would do a lot of these children a world of good, and I don't care if it is at the supermarket or town square. I think that not spanking your child and teaching them discipline and respect for authority is child abuse.

Liberals have tried to take all the unpleasantness out of everyday life, like spanking. We try to rationalize (there is that word again) not spanking by saying it is barbaric and inhumane. We have people in our nation that pretend to live in a utopian society, as if all you have to do is, go on every day and not take any unpleasant action that might upset you or make you unhappy. This is foolhardiness; it is what has brought us behavior-modification drugs. Instead of parents being involved in their children's lives and being active with them or simply letting them go outside and play, they have been convinced by the media that there is an epidemic of attention deficit disorders and hyperactivity disorders. When I was a child, my brothers and I were all hyperactive; that is why my mother let us burn our energy outside playing—after completing our chores and homework, that is. I am not saying that these disorders do not exist; I am, after all, *not* a doctor. I strongly recommend, however, that you get an opinion from two doctors in regards to

ADD. I do think they have been over-diagnosed, and these drugs have been over-prescribed. How is it that a child can have an attention deficit disorder in school, but at home can spend hours in front of the television and recite everything that happened on a television show? Alternatively, how can they sit for hours, play video games, and figure out the quickest routes to the next level? Could it be that, like everyone else, most children have things they find interest in and some things they find boring? It is much easier to focus on things you like than things you dislike. It takes self-discipline. I was taught by my parents to focus on things I find boring. However unpleasant, there are parts of my job I must do. It is hard to focus when I would rather be doing something else. I have no trouble focusing on things I like to do. Some of these children do not have ADD—they have DDD, Discipline Deficit Disorder.

We can continue to make excuses for our shortcomings as parents, or we can take back the right to discipline our children. We owe it to our children to turn them into law–abiding, productive citizens, citizens that have manners and morals. This will help them when they become adults to have happier and more successful lives. We must teach them to stand on their own and quit bailing them out of trouble. Protect them for sure, but allow them to face the music when they do something wrong. In fact, you may want to lead the chorus to make the music a little louder. We cannot continue on the current path that teaches us to be friends with our children. I like to tell my boys that I am their Dad and I will be standing by them long after their friends have abandoned them—standing by them when they are receiving praise and accolades and standing by them when they are taking responsibility for their actions under unpleasant circumstances. Parental involvement should be all-encompassing, chastising bad behavior and applauding the good behavior. There must be a balance. Too much of one and not enough of the other is a recipe for disaster. I think most would find their children would improve in school as well as in other social endeavors.

If you still doubt what I am saying, then try to remember if you have ever heard a child become so unruly in public that they began to scream at the parent, sometimes escalating to vulgar language. Ask yourself, if that had been your parent, what would have happened? Do you think your mom and dad would have made you sit in the "time-out chair"? How often have you seen parents relent to the child's demands in the hope of bargaining for good behavior? Do you really believe that is good for them or you? To elevate a child to a status equal to the parent is highly detrimental to the child's welfare. Their must be a hierarchy in the household. (In my house, it is a monarchy. No votes, no debates, just whatever my queen and I decide.) Unless your child is going to become ruler of the world when they leave home, they must be taught that there will always be an authority to which they must answer. In order to live productively in a civilization, one must be taught civility. The best place for that is in the home, by the people that children should hold in the highest regard. If children do not hold the parents in high regard—the parents that have provided their very livelihood—then how can we expect them to hold a teacher, neighbor, policeman, or judge in high regard, when these people had nothing to do with the child's existence? Furthermore, if the parents do not have the patience and will to control their children, how can they have the audacity to expect someone else to have any patience? Having children is easy; raising them properly, with respect, manners, and decency, is an entirely different matter.

This has been an incremental change over the years that some parents have created, not only for themselves but also even for their neighbors. How often have you heard from your child that the neighbor's child is allowed to do something and been expected to lift your restriction on that particular activity?

Every generation wants their children to be better off than they were. Good parents want their children to be more successful, more educated, more financially secure, and generally happier than they were or are. It is as common as sunlight. Many of these parents worked very hard, sometimes working two jobs in order to do more for their families. These parents should be applauded. Unfortunately, some of them overlooked an ingredient of their persona that helps them to have character as individuals. What ingredient, you may ask? The journey. The hardships that we faced and we seek to remove from our children's lives are part of our character. The difficulties that we faced and conquered have only served to reinforce and support our beliefs. The old saying, "What doesn't kill you will only make you stronger," has more meaning in this regard than most people do realize. Our frugalness comes from our experience of how hard it can be to make money. People who have worked hard to become successful appreciate it more, because they have a personal recollection of what it is like to struggle; they understand the sacrifices necessary to succeed in life. The times of difficulty and struggle are not just knowledge we have; it has been woven into our character. By removing obstacles for our children, we have weakened their resolve. They have not had to face the challenges we faced. They drink ice-cold soda pops out of the refrigerator. We were happy to let the garden hose run until the water-cooled down. It is beyond a child of today's grasp how good they have it, because they have no baseline, in which, to compare their current life. When I was a teenager, my friend purchased, with his own money, a 1963

Volkswagen Bug. It had a standard transmission, and the alternator was bad. It also had no air conditioner. We typically had to push it to get it started. We went everywhere in it, always trying to find a hill on which to park. Children today expect their parents not only to buy them a car, but also to buy them a new or late-model used car. A few years ago, I began to grasp the generation gap and why it occurs. I was watching television one day, an old western with James Stewart, and my son Ryan, then age thirteen, asked me what was wrong with the color on the television. I told him, "Nothing."

He then asked, "Why is it in black and white?"

I laughed and told him, "When I was a real little kid, television shows were all in black and white."

He then asked, "Why?"

I explained that color what not available for television in that era. He was incredulous. He actually thought I was pulling his leg. I then continued to explain to him we only had three networks available to watch (ABC, NBC, and CBS), and in order to be able to change the channel, you actually had to get out of your seat and physically walk over to the television and turn a knob. In fact, you might even have to go outside and turn the antenna until you had a signal. My son could not fathom this and thought it was unbelievable. I also told him that most families that had a television typically only had one. Remember, this was a child that had never experienced life without a remote control. (Next year, I plan to tell him about eight-track tapes.) There will be more advancement in technology in the next twenty years, and his children will find it just as difficult to relate to what they will think was a tough life he had to endure.

The education of our youth is atrocious. We have expanded the curriculum, yet shortened the amount of time in each class. We have reduced our standards for what is an acceptable mark in school. Everyone has heard of "the new math." What is wrong with the old math? It is the same math that Isaac Newton, Albert Einstein, and even the Mayans and Egyptians used; seemed to work for them pretty well. We no longer have as much focus on the three "Rs"—Reading, 'Riting, and 'Rithmetic. We have many children who graduate from high school with a less than adequate level in all these subjects. Yet we are trying to teach Spanish in some second grades and algebra in the seventh grade. Children no longer have the thrill of going to the library and exploring the wonders of reading that only a library can bring. It is much better than booting up a computer and typing in the subject matter.

There will be time for expanded learning for children at ages that are commensurate to their understanding. The necessity for children to completely master the basics has never been more evident than today. If one can read and read well, one can accomplish anything, even if one has no past experience in a particular endeavor. If they can read and comprehend, they can teach themselves how to do something. Ensuring that a child can read is the ultimate gift of real freedom. This cannot be stressed enough: it is better to take the tortoise's approach to education, slow and sure, rather than the fast track of the hare's "hurry up" and not finish the race. It is simply solidifying an educational foundation that will be very strong; then all things will be much easier to learn. This, fortified with returning discipline to schools, will be a starting point to repairing what ails our youth.

Throughout elementary, middle, and high school we must also return to teaching civics and government. This will build an understanding for the electorate of how government is supposed to work. It will help them protect their rights as a nation if they can understand and scrutinize their elected officials.

Disgruntlement #5:
THE ELECTORAL COLLEGE

Congressional leaders as well as the media have maligned the Electoral College—so much so that the people of the country have become confused and frustrated as to why we even use the Electoral College to determine our presidential elections. Typically, the educated elite, the almighty powerful, have once again shown their ignorance or deceit concerning the voting system. Instead of trying to educate the public about it, they take the easier path of calling for its repeal. Never mind the fact that it would take an amendment to the Constitution to do so. Why did the founding fathers create it in the first place? Did they use any foresight at all? Perhaps more than you realize.

In the year 1800, there were only sixteen states in the United States of America. The original thirteen colonies had only increased by three states; those states included Vermont, Kentucky, and Tennessee. To fully comprehend the Electoral College, you must first understand the concerns of the founding fathers and the early members of Congress. To do this, you must further understand the facts as they were and, for the most part, still are. Taking a look at the populations of the sixteen states according to the 1800 Bureau of Census will give us more insight into how the founding fathers and early Congress were thinking.

State Population Senators/Representatives

1. Delaware 64,273 2/1 Total 3
2. Pennsylvania 602,365 2/13 Total 15
3. New Jersey 211,149 2/5 Total 7
4. Georgia 162,686 2/2 Total 4
5. Connecticut 251,002 2/7 Total 9
6. Massachusetts 422,845 2/14 Total 16
7. Maryland 341,548 2/8 Total 10
8. South Carolina 345,591 2/6 Total 8

9. New Hampshire 183,858 2/4 Total 6

10. Virginia 807,557 2/19 Total 21

11. New York 589,051 2/10 Total 12

12. North Carolina 478,103 2/10 Total 12

13. Rhode Island 69,122 2/2 Total 4

14. Vermont 154,465 2/2 Total 4

15. Kentucky 220,955 2/2 Total 4

16. Tennessee 105,602 2/1 Total 3

The concept of bicameral representation in the United States was to help insure that all of its citizens were represented as fairly as possible, regardless of whether you resided in a large, or populous, state or small, or less-populous, state (The Great Compromise of 1787). The House of Representatives and Senate were created to help distribute the representation fairly and equally. The founding fathers knew that some states would be more populated than others, particularly with westward expansion. Still today, even though we are no longer expanding, there are still states with much larger populations than others. Take California and Alaska, for example, California with a population over 36,000,000 and Alaska with a population under 700,000. With the House of Representatives determined by population, this would allow the overall populace of the United States to have a voice in government. However, because some states are more populated than other states, this would potentially allow only a few states to dictate the policy and the direction of the government. If you review our chart, you will see that four states (Virginia, Pennsylvania, Massachusetts, and New York) combined for a total of fifty-six of the one hundred and six representatives, or approximately fifty-three percent of the vote. This potentially could have created a power vacuum, where as many as twelve states might not have a voice in representation at all. The founding fathers knew this would create an intolerable situation. The creation of the Senate and an equal number of senators for each state would ensure a voice for the other twelve states, with a combined Senate member total of twenty-four versus the combined Senate member total of eight for the aforementioned states. This would allow a counterbalance to ensure that the less-populated states that are larger in number than the more populous would have a way to be heard.

Article 2, Section 1 of the U.S. Constitution, determined the first presidents. The electors, one for each state's total number of representatives and senators, would meet in their individual states and vote for two people; these electors made up the Electoral College. Whichever candidate got the most votes was president, and whoever finished second became the vice-president. As you can clearly see, it makes sense that candidates from the most populous states would likely become the presidents. In the first election, George Washington, from Virginia, won the presidency, and, unlike what most people think, did not run unopposed, John Adams, from Massachusetts, finished second. John Adams would finish second again in the next presidential election. He would finally win in the third election, defeating Thomas Jefferson from Virginia. Thomas Jefferson would in turn win the fourth election, defeating Aaron Burr from New York, thus becoming the third president. It was this fourth presidential election that caused quite a stir, as Thomas Jefferson and Aaron Burr tied with seventy-three votes each, while John Adams finished with sixty-five. This caused the House of Representatives to determine the winner. Afterward, the Twelfth Amendment was ratified in 1804, establishing how we elect a president today.

The Electoral College was established so that the less-populous states would also have a voice in presidential elections, in the same manner in which they have a voice in national politics via the senate, by allowing the number of states a candidate carries to have a bearing on the outcome. It is this key element that the political experts and professors miss when they discuss the 2000 presidential election, George W. Bush vs. Albert Gore. There is no disputing that the Democratic nominee, Al Gore, won the popular vote. However, keep in mind that the idea of the bicameral legislature—including the Electoral College, as it was based on the total number of senators and representatives—was to help prevent a lesser number of states from determining the course of this nation simply because they were more populated. George Bush carried 30 states and 271 electoral votes, and Albert Gore carried 20 states and 266 electoral votes. This poses unique questions to the "United" States: How do you stay united if thirty states are disregarded as to how they voted? Should there be a tiebreaker in this situation? If so, isn't the tiebreaker the Electoral College? Is this, perhaps, what the founding fathers had in mind all along, when after the election of 1800, even though ratifying the Twelfth Amendment, they left in place the Electoral College instead of simply making it a popular vote? In 1800, the population was over 4.5 million people; surely, the intelligent people that established this nation were smart enough to consider the odds that a tie in the presidential election would be virtually impossible. Did they leave the Electoral College in place to be a tiebreaker? The presidential election of 1960, John F. Kennedy vs. Richard M. Nixon, may give us some insight. Kennedy won the popular vote by the slimmest of margins (more slim even than of Gore vs. Bush), yet Nixon won more states than Kennedy did. However, in this case, Kennedy won the electoral vote count. Basically, Kennedy won two out of the three. He won the popular vote and the electoral count, while losing the state count. Bush, on the other hand, won the electoral count and the state count while losing the popular vote. It is rare that a candidate does not win all three of these categories. You will not see any media coverage of this anomaly. It is clear that the number of representatives in the House would reflect the population and the number of senators would reflect the number of states. The writers of the Twelfth Amendment wanted the electoral count to reflect in some measure the number of states a candidate carried as well as the popular vote. They could have left two electoral votes per state out of the Electoral College tally if they were only concerned with the popular vote. If this were the case, subtracting 60 votes from George Bush would have left him with 211 electoral votes, while subtracting 40 votes from Albert Gore would have left him with 226 electoral votes. It is as clear as the nose on one's face that the intention was to consider the state count as well as the popular count. Demonstrating two different instances where Kennedy or Bush did not win all three categories (popular count, state count, and electoral count). Both men were elected, one a Democrat and one a Republican. If you look at the elections, you will see both similarities and differences. The different parties will still cry foul in the elections, the Democrats crying foul about the 2000 election and the Republicans crying foul about the 1960 election. It is almost like watching a sporting event when your favorite team benefits from an obscure rule and wins. That, of course is okay; however, with the shoe on the other foot, that is a very different matter. The political parties will always choose the side that benefits them the most at that particular time. They will later change opinions when it is conducive to promoting the particular agenda of the day. They do not want people to realize the Electoral College worked perfectly in the 2000 election, just as it was intended to over two hundred years ago when Congress chose not to alter it with the Twelfth Amendment.

So what is the major difference between the early congressional leaders of the United States and congressional leaders of today? Most of the early congressional leaders were more concerned with the citizens, unlike the congressional leaders of today that seem more consumed with their own ambition and power. An opposite of this can be demonstrated by looking at the election of 1800. The election being tied required the House of Representatives to determine the winner. Alexander Hamilton, a Federalist that convinced his party to vote for Thomas Jefferson over Aaron Burr.

This was done, in Hamilton's view, for the good of the nation. He did not particularly like either Jefferson or Burr. Hamilton was a longtime political adversary of both men. He saw Burr as being too ambitious to be President of the United States. Even though he disagreed with Jefferson on most issues, he supported him over Burr and convinced enough of his party to do the same. The outgoing Federalist Party could have blocked the election of either man, as they held the majority in the House. It was also well known that Alexander Hamilton did not personally like either person. Seldom today would you see this type of leadership demonstrated by members of either party. The founding fathers and the early members of Congress were some of the brightest minds in the world. Even though there were only 106 representatives and 32 senators, they seemed to have had a higher combined intellectual quotient than the 435 representatives and 100 senators we have today.

There are many people in the country, including those in the media, which relish the opportunity to debate the separation of church and state, using a quote from Thomas Jefferson concerning the wall of separation of church and state. However, they never seem to quote Thomas Jefferson about a pure democracy: "A democracy is nothing more than mob rule, where fifty-one percent of the people take away the rights of the other forty-nine." If we elected a president strictly on popular vote, this would be exactly the case.

I guess there are those that only like to quote famous people when it is convenient to their particular cause. (Fast forward to Disgruntlement #9.)

Disgruntlement #6:
PARTY AFFILIATION AND PERSUASION

In the interest of full disclosure, I will again affirm that I am a conservative. I believe in a strict adherence to the Constitution of the United States. It is true that more Republicans are conservative than are liberal. Furthermore, it is true that more Democrats are liberal than are conservative. It seems extremely confusing sometimes, trying to figure out who best represents your interest. Republicans that are liberal are referred to as moderates. You never hear of a Democrat being called moderate. I suppose it is because conservative Democrats are known as "blue dog" Democrats. Wouldn't it be nice if the parties were simply identified as "The Conservative Party," "The Liberal Party," or "The Moderate Party"? (The Moderate Party would also be known as "The 'I can't seem to figure out what I stand for' Party," or better yet, "The Wishy-Washy Party.")

The Moderate Republican:

Once known as the Rockefeller Republicans, the rich elitists in the Republican Party were the movers and shakers of the nation. Their main goal was power and securing more wealth for themselves. This type of self-interest was what led to the rebirth of the Democratic Party under President Franklin D. Roosevelt and the idea that Democrats were for the common person. It is a belief that is still held by many people to this day.

The so-called moderate Republicans would like you to believe they are independent thinkers. Nothing could be further from the truth. They seek to sit on the fence and pander to both sides, picking and choosing the most popular trend of the day in order to convince the electorate they are above the debating and squabbling. You will never see a moderate Republican take an adamant stance on anything. How would it be possible to consider with great intensity anything and not have a staunch opinion one way or another?

Moderate Republicans seek to live in the gray areas of politics, never quite defining black or white. If you think with all your heart that you are right, you must not be afraid to walk upstream. Moderate Republicans choose the coward's way out; this is why there are no moderates defined as great leaders. The very definition of "leader" eliminates those who are cowards. Consider the first Republican president, President Abraham Lincoln very conservative, yet regarded still today as one of our greatest presidents. On the liberal side, President Thomas Jefferson is also considered one of our greatest presidents. Moderates are sometimes elected president; however, they are never considered great, because even though they were presidents they were only leaders in title, not in their actions or beliefs.

These moderate Republicans should take some advice from President Abraham Lincoln: "You can fool all of the people some of the time, and some of the people all of the time, but you cannot fool all of the people all of the time." This statement epitomizes the moderate.

The "Blue Dog" Democrat:

These Democrats should also be known as "throwback" Democrats. These are the Democrats that your fathers and grandfathers were accustomed to vote for. These Democrats are in the mold of another great president, President Harry S. Truman. These are the Democrats that the Democratic Party leadership would like to silence, or at least to contain. They honor traditional moral and family values and are largely from the southern states. When you talk to the older generation and they tell you that the Democrat Party is the party that looks out for the common person, these are the Democrats the elders think still represent the entire party. Unfortunately, the elder generation, in many cases, does not even know they are merely a minority wing of the party. Because of this, you will also hear the term "yellow dog Democrat," meaning simply that a Democrat will vote for a yellow dog provided it has the (D) after his/her name. The "Blue Dogs" once dominated the Democrat Party in both the House of Representatives and the Senate, swept in when Roosevelt was elected and often today aligning themselves with the Republican Party on social and moral issues.

The Liberal Democrat:

They are diligent promoters of policies taxing the wealthy or big business (under the guise of looking out for the common person) in order to create programs to purchase votes from the poor. They believe that if you have the financial means for more than just you and your family, you should be forced by taxation to relinquish some of it in order to support the less fortunate with a greater need.* They believe that big government is the answer to all the nation's ills, from social problems to economic problems. They feel there is nothing the government cannot take care of. ** The Liberal Democrats try to create a co-dependence between the less fortunate and government. On the surface, this seems kind and caring; unfortunately, the less fortunate always remain less fortunate and never climb out of the dependence hole that has been dug for them by the people who claim to be helping them. This is why liberals are "surface thinkers"***: they look at a problem, but only see the surface. They make all kinds of attempts to fix the problem on the surface, but few attempts are made to look beneath the surface of a problem to see what lies below. It can be compared to someone who would shear the tops off of icebergs, then think the ocean free of them, only to ensure that a disaster like the *Titanic* becomes even more likely than before—whereas if they had taken the initiative to look below the surface, they would have realized there was a bigger problem at hand and the quick fix would only make things worse.

*If you wonder what could possibly be wrong with that philosophy, then perhaps you should be advised that was a summarization of the following quote: "From each according to his ability, to each according to his need" (Karl Marx, 1875).

** This is the philosophy of communism: that the state will provide all things for its people.

***Unfortunately, many do not know they are only "surface thinkers."

The Conservative Republican:

True conservatives believe in the power of the people in all aspects of life. They believe that freedom is the ultimate gift for everyone. They, in turn, believe in a strict interpretation of the Constitution to insure that freedom will always remain for many generations to come. They believe diluting the Constitution in one area dilutes it in all areas. They have a foundation that can only support framework built on that foundation; any variance or overreaching of that foundation will cause a failure in the structure and a collapse of grave proportions upon itself. They do not confuse freedom with "living free and doing whatever you want, without responsibility." On the contrary, they believe that with freedom comes enormous responsibility, not only to oneself and in one's actions, but responsibility to others as well. They believe that smaller, less intrusive government is essential, to promoting true freedom. They also believe in the old saying, "Give a man a fish, and he will eat for a day; teach a man to fish, and he will eat for a lifetime" (author unknown).

The terms *liberal* and *conservative* as defined in the political realm are easy enough, liberal meaning a broad interpretation of the constitution and conservative meaning a strict interpretation of the constitution. That is really the definition; it sounds simple enough. Many will say the broader the view, the better for the American people. However, you must remember, the U.S. Constitution was written to limit government power and authority of government over the individual; by broadening the interpretation, you in essence broaden the reach of government. This nation was founded on the individual and the rights of the individual. It is communist countries that seek to limit the achievements and rights of the individual. When we begin to encroach upon the freedoms and rights of the individual, we begin to erode the ideals of this nation.

Disgruntlement #7:
THE FAIRNESS DOCTRINE

The word *fair* is defined as being done without bias and therefore reasonable and impartial.

The word, even though it has a clear and concise definition, has been made to be a relative term by the user, according to the individual opinion of the observer. Each person has his/her own standards of "fair" and "unfair," many times adjusting their opinion on how they feel, losing focus on the actual meaning of the word. Over the last several years, some in this country have embarked on a journey to seek out the unfairness of life and make efforts to correct it. A novel idea; regrettably, they have missed the boat entirely. The only thing that needs to be equal and fair as possible is opportunity; everyone should have equal opportunities. I say "as fair as possible" because, to be completely fair, every one of us would have to have the exact same circumstances as everyone else, and that is impossible. However, there are those among us that want more. There are some that feel that it is only fair if every opportunity ends in success, with no regard for possible failure. This would ultimately take away thrill of success. What really makes success so great is that failure is so bad. Why try your best to succeed when failing will bring you the same reward? If fairness is what is being sought, how is it fair for someone who pays their dues and makes sacrifices to accomplish whatever their goal might be to have their efforts wiped away by elevating someone who did not make those same sacrifices or pay those same dues and awarding them that same goal? The cold, hard truth is that we all have differences: some are smart, some are tall, some are good-looking, and some are strong. Reality will demonstrate to all that not only do people not look the same, but also they do not have the same abilities. This is actually a good thing. It may seem unfair on the "surface," but underneath the surface, you will find that it allows for the creation of different achievements and different thoughts, which in turn allows for different art, different poetry, different music, and a wide variety of differences for society. I have always challenged my children as I was challenged, with the motto, "Dare to be different." Some of the suggestions and efforts made by the "Fairness Society" are very shameful and utterly ridiculous. Yet they have been able to gain support from the feeble-minded that seek to demonstrate their goodness in this misguided and silly idea. How boring a world it would be if all people were the same. On one hand, the "Fairness Society" speaks of diversity. (Diversity means variety of something. Must they be educated on everything?) How can you have a variety if everyone and their achievements are the same? My youngest son was born with severe birth defects. I wish he had not been born this way. It is hard sometimes to watch his older twin brother play sports without feeling sad for the younger sibling not being able to participate. However, the answer is not to disallow my older twin son from participating in sports. The solution was to help my youngest son find a life that makes him happy, and he has taught me more about myself that I might not have ever known. I am as proud of him, as I am of all my children. I could not love him any more than I do. We have to learn to accept all people for who they are. Yes, we must do our very best to protect and ensure *equal opportunity* for everyone, but not by denying other people the successes they have rightfully earned.

I like sports; I watch football, basketball, baseball, tennis, golf, bowling (my favorite pastime), and a variety of others as well. When I was in high school, I would have liked to have played basketball. I would like to play professional basketball today. Unfortunately, I suffer from height deficit disorder, as well as speed deficit disorder. In other words, I am not tall enough to play center or forward, and I am too slow to play guard. I have been considering taking the NBA to court for having such stringent requirements to play as a professional. It is not my fault; I am not physically equipped to perform at the standards necessary. Something should be done about this. Let's place a call to the "Fairness Society." The truth is that even if I had the opportunity, I would still not be playing in the NBA, because I am not good enough. I would have failed in my opportunity. I was not good enough to play in high school either. I could not have even played for the high school girls' team. (That sounds worse than it really is because our girls' team was number one in the state three out of the four years I attended high school and second the other year. As a matter of fact, the coach of the girls' team my freshman year was Van Chancellor, former coach of the Houston Comets and current coach of the LSU Lady Tigers.) Nevertheless, I am not ashamed; I am who I am. Perhaps if the "Fairness Society" put more interest in helping people be comfortable with who they are, these people would not feel slighted and could pursue endeavors that would bring them satisfaction and a feeling of accomplishment. The truth is; there are many things at which I do not excel, even things at which I try my best. If we teach our children to strive to be the best they can be, then even if they finish second, third, or dead last, it does not matter as long as they tried their best. I would love the opportunity at forty-five years old to play against Michael Jordan, Lebron James, Larry Bird, Magic Johnson, and a lot more superstars that would take too long to name. I would lose; I would be stomped into the ground. I would try my very best, but it would not matter. I would not want to be spotted any points, mind you, nor would I want them to take it easy on me; merely to compete and play with people of so much talent would be satisfaction enough. I would leave the court with my head held high and pride in my heart as long as I tried my best.

We teach our children that they can do anything if they put their minds to it. That is a good philosophy and an attitude that should be commended. However, it should not be taken literally. Sometimes there are physical attributes that one must possess in order complete one's goal. These attributes are God-given and are gifts to those who possess them. Each one of us is endowed with our own talents and abilities; it is only a matter of finding them within ourselves. Once we do find them, we must exploit them to the fullest degree. I know that I will never be a hero on the basketball court, on the football field, or even in the science lab. I can be a hero to my children, my wife, and even my friends by just being myself. Do not insult the character of those that do not excel in one endeavor or another by trying to even the playing field. Athletes who were experiencing a temporary handicap performed two of the most inspirational performances I have ever seen. In 1976, when boxing at the Olympic trials, Sugar Ray Leonard had calcium deposits in one of his hands, so he basically could only box with one hand. The performance was truly inspirational. He went on to win, and I became a big fan, not just, because he was great boxer, but because he showed so much character and determination by not giving up even when the odds were against him. In my mind, that was only topped by Keri Scruggs. The courage she had to have had to even attempt that vault, let alone execute it perfectly, in the Olympics was unbelievable. I still marvel at it today. I still use it as inspiration for myself, and I tell others about it that are too young to have seen it. Fairness is simply making sure the opportunities are the same for everyone. What an individual does with the opportunities they are presented is completely up to them.

The frustration that the "Fairness Society" experiences is due to the harsh reality that some of these opportunities are presented at such a young age that many are not wise enough to take advantage of them. (Go back and re-read "Disgruntlement #4: Today's Youth" for solutions.) Because children have been allowed to make decisions not based on experience and wisdom, they suffer the consequences of the poor choices they make. I know of many people without a high school education that do not want their children to make the same mistake. They do this because; they love their children and have the benefit of experience concerning the result. These parents have learned that life is not fair and want their children to have every advantage possible. (Even those without a high school diploma want their children to have an advantage.) Hello, "Fairness Society," do you get the picture?

The "Fairness Society" has even gotten itself mixed up in news coverage by the networks. Apparently, liberals (who, by the way, make up the "Fairness Society") have a problem with the FOX News Channel not being fair. I watch a variety of news channels and do not see the problem. I do see that liberals are questioned equally as much as conservatives on the programs. Perhaps this is much more than they are accustomed to on the other networks.

A Special Report w/Brit Hume:

The news is covered, and then they have a segment called "The Grapevine," in which typically four guests participate. Regulars include Fred Barnes (conservative) Mort Kondracki (liberal), Mara Liason (liberal), and Juan Williams (liberal); there are others from time to time that replace the regulars. Brit Hume does an excellent job reining in both sides when necessary. He asks equally hard questions of all. The funny thing is that as although I am a conservative, my favorite regular is Mort Kondracki, a liberal. I think he tries to give the most forthright answers.

The Bill O'Rielly Show:

Bill, in my mind, is an independent. I agree with a lot of what he says and disagree with him sometimes. That is fine; I still enjoy the show. I have seen segments of the show, and the following day he will read e-mails from viewers regarding that particular segment. Sometimes he reads an ultra-liberal e-mail from a viewer that accuses him of being a spokesperson for the Bush administration, and then he immediately reads an e-mail regarding that same story from an ultra-conservative that accuses him of being a mouthpiece of the DNC. I find it amusing. I also find it amusing in light of this that any viewer would say that he does not toe an independent line.

Hannity & Colmes:

Sean Hannity (conservative) and Alan Colmes (liberal) share the show, each questioning the people being interviewed. They themselves are biased, but as a team, they provide equal representation of both viewpoints.

These are the political programs available on FOX News Channel in primetime. I am at a loss to understand what the liberals Sen. Hillary Clinton (D), Sen. Ted Kennedy (D), and many others are fussing about. The truth is, liberals are not used to being asked tough questions on CNN, MSNBC, NBC, ABC, and certainly not CBS—just ask Dan Rather. It is all according to perspective. The senators again, demonstrating that they are "surface thinkers," believe that if you do not like the message, you should shoot the messenger. They complain about Rupert Murdoch, the owner of the FOX Network, buying too many media outlets and reaching viewers with politically neutral coverage. The senators have never complained of the New York *Times,* with a daily circulation of over one million and a Sunday circulation over one and a half million, having a political slant. The New York *Times* also publishes fifteen newspapers. Where is the outcry of the "Fairness Society"?

As you can see, the "Fairness Society" is only concerned with results *they* deem fair, which has no bearing on what actually is fair, and it never will. In the time of the Soviet Union, the ruling class determined that it was unfair for some to have advantages that others did not have. The Communist solution: make everyone that is not among the political elite the same. They determined what was fair and unfair and fixed it—they made it unfair for everyone.

Disgruntlement #8:
THE MINIMUM WAGE AND TAXES

Who is fooling whom, anyway? The "surface thinkers" have struck again. While pandering to the poor and the uneducated, they keep the poor and uneducated from ever improving their lives. This requires propaganda from the left that poor people of the United States need a higher minimum wage. They claim you cannot raise a family on minimum wage. This assertion is absolutely correct. You cannot and never will be able to. Many of the people in this nation go along with it because they will feel better about themselves. The following chart will illustrate how much the minimum wage has helped the employees making the minimum wage. It will also substantiate what was asserted in the foreword: that politicians have no clue what everyday items cost. The chart will show the cost of a gallon of milk and a carton of eggs every year the minimum wage went up and how much of the hour an individual had to work in those respective years.

Year	Minimum Wage	Cost of a Gallon of Milk	Total Work Required to Purchase Milk	Cost of a Carton of Eggs	Total Work Required to Purchase Eggs
1975	$2.10	$1.57	44min 54sec	$0.77	36min 40sec
1976	$2.30	$1.65	43min 02sec	$0.84	36min 31sec
1978	$2.65	$1.71	38min 43sec	$0.82	30min 56sec
1979	$2.90	$1.62	33min 30sec	$0.85	29min 19sec
1980	$3.10	$2.16	41min 48sec	$0.91	29min 21sec
1981	$3.35	$2.22	39min 45sec	$0.90	26min 52sec
1990	$3.80	$2.78	43min 53sec	$1.00	26min 19sec
1991	$4.25	$2.80	39min 31sec	$1.01	23min 46sec
1996	$4.75	$3.30	41min 40sec	$1.31	27min 34sec
1997	$5.15	$3.22	37min 31sec	$1.17	22min 43sec
2007	$5.85	$4.19	42min 58sec	$ 1.80	17min 35 sec
*Average time per hour			40min 40sec		N/A

*In June of 2007 milk was $3.78 at the local Walmart, while minimum wage was $5.15. It took 44 minutes and 2 seconds to purchase a gallon of milk after minimum wage took effect.

**this chart is for education purposes only. It has been figured from gross income alone.

In actuality, the amount of tax one pays would also affect how much one would have to work; however, it would be impossible to calculate the tax each individual might pay based on deductions. It will do, however, for our purpose of a general study.

With the increase of minimum wage to $5.85 per hour, the kind, always-caring "surface thinkers" have allowed the minimum wage earners to work one minute and four seconds less per hour to be able to afford that gallon of milk. Now with the help of these "surface thinkers," the minimum wage earner will have an extra ten cents per hour to spend on other needs. If they are frugal, they will have an extra eighty cents a day. The minimum wage has done very little to help the poor. The chart unequivocally illustrates that every time the minimum wage goes up, so does the price of milk. At least eggs have dropped in price. (This is primarily due to an increase in poultry farms over the years.) The price goes up because these goods do not get on the grocer's shelf automatically; someone has to be paid to work the various jobs getting them there. The chart further illustrates that over the past thirty-two years, the average work time needed to in order to afford a gallon of milk is forty minutes and forty seconds. If you raise the minimum wage to

$10.00 per hour, a gallon of milk would cost $6.73 per gallon; at $15.00 per hour of work, the cost is $10.10 per gallon. The price of things increases as minimum wage goes up. The problem of poverty has not been resolved, and never will be, by merely raising the minimum wage. You must raise the education level of the impoverished so that they may obtain jobs that pay more than minimum wage, or the circle will never be broken. Many people making the minimum wage are high-school dropouts and/or have police records. More and more companies are requiring police checks and drug screening as a precondition to employment. Some even require some academic testing, with the good jobs naturally going to the more educated.

If someone was making $12.00 per hour in June 2007, he/she was making $6.85 more than minimum wage. He/she obviously has earned his/her way up the ladder in wage and would like to stay $6.85 above minimum wage. Paying that individual $12.70 per hour would seem to be an easy solution, and probably most would be happy. The minimum-wage earners do not realize that everyone else wants a raise too. Understandably, many people have worked hard to get where they are in life. This also helps ensure that prices increase and the cost of living goes up, ensuring that minimum-wage earners never climb out of the dire straits in which they find themselves. Let us investigate further: consider for a moment that an individual did get a raise and is happy to continue making the same amount more than the minimum-wage worker. On the other hand, did he/she actually get a raise? Twelve dollars per hour is 233% more than five dollars and fifteen cents per hour, while twelve dollars and seventy cents per hour is 217% more than five dollars and eighty-five cents per hour. Have you ever wondered why your dollar does not go as far as it used too? We have all heard the phrase, "The rich get richer and the poor get poorer." You probably never stopped to really consider why; this is why, and it is not the Rich's doing—it is the pandering politicians' doing. They will never tell you that if they make minimum wage $100.00 per hour, a gallon of milk will more than likely cost $67.33. That does not sound so bad, except most of your change will be spent purchasing the $22.43 carton of eggs.

All wages are based from the bottom up, from the lowest to the highest. This is how many union contracts are negotiated: when minimum wage goes up, so does the union wage. There are more people in the unions than are on minimum wage. Who really got the benefit of the wage increase? Which politicians are receiving the most contributions from the unions? The union members have a desire to make a certain amount over minimum wage too. Again, understandably, poor people are not the only ones who do not want to be poor. How do we combat this problem? Education is the key. We must educate our youth so they will be able to break the cycle of poverty. There will be those that refuse, and they will be relegated to poverty for most, if not all, of their lives. If a person wants to improve his/her circumstances, perhaps second-chance programs could be set up to further one's education in a vocational skill or possibly a degree. We could use some of the money we save on education. (See "Disgruntlement #2: Congress and Our Money.")

If someone is a millionaire and already has plenty of money, which is in liquid assets, they are not affected by a depression. In fact, if they have all liquid assets and the prices drop, they can actually afford more things than before. However, most wealthy people do not have all of their assets in liquid form. They have them invested and have just as much at stake in the economy as everyone else—probably more. Because they have their money invested, the investments they have made help secure employment for the entire population. When politicians claim wealthy individuals and corporations need to be taxed more, you must consider the following. Wealthy individuals and corporations are in a position, in most cases, to pass the tax increase off to the consumer. (That is us!) For instance, millions of individuals invest in corporations in the hope of profiting from their investments. If a corporation has to pay ten million dollars more in taxes, it simply increases the price of the goods or services it provides. Who pays the additional tax? The consumer, that is who. (That is us, again!) Who do you think is more concerned about the price of a gallon of milk: a minimum-wage earner or a millionaire? When a working-class individual is expecting a tax refund, they start to consider what they might use it for: perhaps a vacation, new car, or other expenditure. Do you think that Bill Gates is sitting around waiting on his refund check to go on vacation? Of course not. Have you ever run into Ted Turner at Walmart? Of course not. When you raise taxes on the wealthy and corporations, they have to come up with the money through income, and that means price increases. They want to make more money than the previous year; this is understandable, as we all do, and as the investors in the corporations do as well. An investor cannot make money if the corporation he/she has invested in loses money. Some of you may even be investors yourself; so in essence, you want the prices raised on yourself as well. Politicians do their utmost to talk around these facts in order to garner support from the working class to attack the wealthy class. The working class needs to realize they are only attacking themselves in the end.

The class warfare some politicians promote by recommending programs to pander the middle class and the poor is actually making poor people have less. It also makes them dependent upon these politicians for their existence. All Americans should be given an opportunity to be free and live free. Rampant taxation will only destroy the economy because it reduces the amount of money invested in this country. These investments are critical to national employment. These investments create higher-paying jobs for the middle class and even the poor. Government handouts may treat the symptoms of poverty, but they do not cure the disease of poverty.

Disgruntlement #9:
SEPARATION OF CHURCH AND STATE

The discussion of such a topic will require a visit back to the Declaration of Independence, the United States Constitution, and other historical documents. Most Americans are ill informed about what exactly "separation of church and state" means. First of all, the term is not in the U.S. Constitution but, as we cited earlier in "Disgruntlement #1: The Media," the First Amendment, first phrase: "Congress shall make no law respecting the establishment of religion, or prohibiting the free exercise thereof…." The question is whether the intent was to totally remove religion from government or government from religion, or both. The whole concept of the separation of church and state originates from a letter from then-President Thomas Jefferson to the Danbury Baptist Association dated January 1, 1802, in response to the letter received from the Danbury Baptist Association dated October 7, 1801. The letter from the Danbury Baptist Association was seeking the president's view of the First Amendment, specifically in reference to religion. Before we examine the letters, let us first examine a few historical facts. Thomas Jefferson took no part in writing the U.S. Constitution, as he was an ambassador to France; he was not even in the country when it was ratified. He did not—as James Madison, Alexander Hamilton, and John Jay, via the Federalist Papers, did—work diligently on its passage. He was not present during the ratification of the Bill of Rights, which contains the First Amendment. He did, however, write the Declaration of Independence. He is rightly considered one of the founding fathers. It is because of this that his opinion was sought and considered to this very day. In the Declaration of Independence, Jefferson started the second paragraph with the statement, "We hold these truths to be self-evident, that all men are created equal, that they are endowed by their Creator, with certain *unalienable* Rights, that among these are Life, Liberty, and the pursuit of Happiness..." Jefferson had stated that a higher authority, the Creator of man, in essence saying these rights were granted by God and could not be taken away, ordained the unalienable rights. However, in the U.S. Constitution, the Bill of Rights addresses freedom of religion *without* the same proclamation, i.e. that freedom of religion is an unalienable right granted by the Creator. It is somewhat vague, and for that exact reason, the. They indicated in their letter, they believed, rightly, that religion was a matter between God and the individual. The reply, in which President Jefferson concurred in the second paragraph of his letter, is where the debate of separation of church and state begins.

First of all, since Thomas Jefferson took no part in writing or ratifying the U.S. Constitution, he could have in no way known the intent of the writers. His interpretation is no different from any other president's opinion regarding the U.S. Constitution. He never served in the capacity of a Supreme Court justice, and his opinion should have no bearing before the high court. All he was doing was giving his opinion to a group of individuals. It is still possible the Supreme Court could have developed the same opinion on their own? However, any time there is a ruling on the separation of church and state, the high court invariably refers back to this letter to bail them out. Quoting the opinion of the third president and treating it with the same reverence and respect as the U.S. Constitution is ludicrous. To do that would be tantamount to allowing any successor to the office of president the same influence over the U.S. Constitution, a duty that belongs to the Supreme Court itself.

Consider that after Thomas Jefferson wrote the Declaration of Independence, he did not merely send it off to the British Crown with his signature alone; fifty-six representatives signed it. They were in concurrence with the document; they even added a laundry list of complaints to it. By contrast, there were thirty-eight representatives that signed the U.S. Constitution. Not one of those thirty-eight was Thomas Jefferson. When discussing freedom of religion and the original intent of the First Amendment, it would seemingly be more prudent to discuss the views of the first four chief justices of the Supreme Court: John Jay, John Rutledge, Oliver Ellsworth, and John Marshall—in fact, particularly John Rutledge, as he was one of the signers of the U.S. Constitution. The wall of separation that President Jefferson interpreted while serving as president is only that—an interpretation. Was it wrong, or was it right? It certainly was controversial. Perhaps the writers of the U.S. Constitution purposely left the First Amendment, in regards to religion, vague so that each citizen could draw their own interpretation without the influence of government.

The "separation of church and state" has been debated for many years and will be debated for many more to come. Just exactly what does it mean? The phrase is just as vague as the First Amendment: does it *only* apply to the federal government being restricted from establishing a national religion? Or does it apply to no faith or religion being demonstrated on government property? The Supreme Court, quoting Thomas Jefferson, has ruled in favor of the latter. Is demonstrating one's religious beliefs on federal property an infraction of freedom of religion? Is imposing laws preventing the demonstration of religious beliefs on federal property an infringement on freedom of speech? The Supreme Court itself has the Ten Commandments displayed not only on its doors, but also above the bench. Is it simply a matter of sharing space among different religions? Or put simply; matter of tolerance, perhaps, around this country? Everyone is afraid of having his or her personal religious views trampled. The feeling that seeing someone demonstrate his or her religious beliefs somehow infringes upon yours is ludicrous. Everyone is entitled to their own personal relationship with their God. Will we all allow our religious beliefs to be relegated to private ceremonies just so we do not have to see someone else's? I once saw a Moslem man pray, and I have also seen a Jewish man pray. Did observing this make me less of a Christian? I think not. Believe it or not, it made me more steadfast in my beliefs. There is much selfishness throughout the country—so much so that many will abandon their right to display their religion just so no one else can display theirs. This is the epitome of selfishness. I would tend to think one common thread in all religions is kindness and selflessness. Instead, many are permanently engaged in religious segregation. The government's implementation of this segregation will only escalate into further frustration. I do not personally know any Christians that want to quash other people's religious viewpoints. They do wish to have equal opportunity to display their own religious viewpoints. Many of the people that protest against religious expression are simply those attempting to get their fifteen minutes of fame.

Today, Americans debate about swearing an oath. Some say it must be done on the Bible. Swearing an oath on the Bible does not compel someone to tell the truth (consider all the people convicted of perjury), although some people may feel more compelled to tell the truth based on their individual religious beliefs. We often hear people say, "I swear on everything I hold dear" or "I swear on my mother's grave." What good would it do for person A to swear on what person B holds dear, or to swear on person B's mother's grave? How would that add any credibility to what person A was saying? It would not. When someone is taking an oath, it is better to let that person, if they so choose, swear on something of value to them, not you. If a

Jewish person wants to swear on the Tanakh, or if a Moslem chooses to swear on the Koran, we must remember it is their oath. Whatever they may choose to swear on must have value to them, not necessarily you.

The most interesting thing about this country is that many people traveled across the Atlantic so they might express their religious views in public without persecution. They founded communities and expressed themselves openly. That right was to be protected under the freedom of speech and the right to assemble. Yet the government, in an attempt to regulate this religious freedom to protect everyone else, has stirred up more controversy than it has settled. Where will it end? If I see a cross on top of the steeple of the church from my home, is that infringement? What if the sun creates a shadow of the cross on my yard? If I see the Star of David on the synagogue as I drive by, is that also infringement?

Many times, we overlook the obvious, then immerse ourselves in self–righteousness, then become too blind to see beyond our own desires and wishes. We seek to extinguish the rights of all those that are different, sometimes contrary to our own moral beliefs, as if the end will justify the means. What if someone founded democracy as a religion? What if the U.S. Constitution was that religion's holy book? We could have the Republican Tabernacle Choir and appoint Democrat Deacons. Would we have to ban the practice of democracy in all federal buildings? I seek to be facetious so that others may see that freedom of religion is between every individual and his/her God. That is the main topic that is missed by so many in Thomas Jefferson's famous letter to the Danbury Baptist Association. "Believing with you that religion is a matter that lies solely between man and his God that he owes account to none other for his faith or his worship." The word *none* was specifically referring to the government. Ironically, the government may have done exactly what Thomas Jefferson was against.

Disgruntlement #10:
IMMIGRATION REFORM?

This title immediately brings to light the idea that reform is a misnomer; it should be immigration enforcement. We have many laws concerning illegal immigration. What most Americans want is for them to be enforced. That seems to be a rather reasonable request from the citizens of this country. Once again, there is a lack of proper representation from Congress. Why? Votes, this is the only reason. Do not be fooled by all the touchy-feely nonsense that many of those that are supposed to be running government are perpetrating on the legal citizens of this country. They could not care less about the illegal immigrants personally. It is about votes and nothing more. Many of them have studied the voter demographics in states like California, Texas, New York, and Florida. These states have a large Hispanic influence. It is that voter influence that inhibits Congress from taking decisive action. The Latino vote is the fastest growing demographic in the United States. Let us look at the electoral vote count of the aforementioned states: California fifty-five, Texas thirty-four, New York thirty-one, and Florida twenty-seven. One hundred forty-seven electoral votes of the two hundred seventy needed to win if you throw in Arizona's ten and New Mexico's five, that is fifteen more for a grand total of one hundred sixty-two, or sixty percent of the electoral votes need to win the presidency. These states also provide one hundred fifty of the four hundred thirty-five House seats and twelve of the Senate seats. We need look no further when trying to figure out why this is a difficult issue on which to get any laws with teeth in them passed through the legislature. The government is basically again using our tax money to buy votes. The government spends enormous amounts of money on the illegal immigrants that are here, from education to medical costs, while at the same time getting no tax money from these people. The entire burden for illegal immigration is entirely on the backs of U.S. citizens. The government knows the solution, yet they sit by and watch the American taxpayer be taken advantage of. When you consider the cost of social services, incarceration, and education that the government spends on illegal immigrants, it breaks down to approximately $500 per year for every man, woman, and child that is a legal citizen in this country. Ask yourself, how long does it take you to come up with your share of that burden? How hard do you have to work in order to come up with $500? Would you not prefer to spend that money on your immediate family? This bill will only increase as the years go by. Each year, you will have to work harder and harder to support the ineptness of our Congress, as each year, illegal immigration becomes more and more costly. The money we would save on illegal immigration would by itself wipe out the budget deficit in four years. We could then begin to start paying the national debt. Many people would argue that the expense of deporting illegal immigrants would be great. They, of course, would be correct—all investments require an initial payment—but the money we would save far outweighs the cost of continuous increases in taxpayer money being spent each year on illegal immigration. Critics will try to make the argument again that we must be more compassionate, that we cannot see people turned away for medical care, food, or education. I actually agree, considering we are not savages. However, the question that American citizens need to be asking is, why has the government allowed it to get to that point? Critics will try to point the finger of blame at the citizens that are tired of paying the burden, calling them mean and heartless. This will be done, of course, to obfuscate the real issue: if the illegal immigrant was not here in the U.S. in the first place, if our government had done its job, the concerned citizens would not be in the position of looking like the bad guys. Congress once again spends the taxpayers' money with little regard for how hard people have to work to earn that money. There are many things working families sacrifice and deny themselves because they cannot afford them. It is a slap in the faces of all those that live from paycheck to paycheck for the government to simply spend it freely, without any consideration of its citizens. Five hundred dollars per person; perhaps someone would not have had to work as hard to get those much-needed car repairs, or a new water heater for the house, or the down payment on a child's braces—this list could go on and on. Regardless of what the critics would say, ask them only this question. If a person works to support his/her family, is it really selfishness if the person wants to spend his/her money on their family instead of someone else's family?

People that choose to migrate to this country legally should be welcome and even applauded. However, they must follow the proper channels to become legal citizens. For all of our problems, this nation is still the best place to live in the world. It should be noted that many people come from Mexico and other Latin American countries legally and illegally because there is not an abundance of well-paying jobs in their respective countries. Most come here as a matter of survival. These countries, however, are sovereign nations; they must deal with the problems of their citizens. The United States has been a crutch to these countries for allowing this rampant illegal immigration. There is no reason for these countries to repair their employment problems, as most of those that are dissatisfied have left their respective countries. If decent-paying jobs were abundant in the countries, most would stay home and never consider crossing the border illegally. Some of these countries even promote illegal immigration to the U.S. because many of their citizens will send money back to their individual families, thus helping to bolster the economies of these countries. According to immigration research, over forty billion dollars has been wired to Mexico from illegal immigrants since January 2006. This parasitic relationship is endangering the economy of the United States, while Congress sits by and watches. All of its members have sworn an oath to protect and defend the United States and her citizens. Congress must be made to recognize that oath and take it seriously as well.

New laws may be required to help enforce our existing laws. Employers that are willing to hire illegal immigrants must have tougher fines and face longer prison sentences. If many people are coming to this country for jobs, we must make the jobs unavailable for those that would cross the border illegally. Potential employers and current employers must be made to understand it is not conducive to their own freedom or to their wallets to hire illegal immigrants. These unscrupulous employers must be held accountable, as they are as much a part of the problem as the illegal immigrants. Furthermore, fines and prison terms may need to be raised for those who would forge documentation to show legal standing for illegal immigrants as well. The problem cannot be properly addressed by simply deporting illegal immigrants. The enticement for illegal immigration must be removed.

The unions have a hidden agenda: while publicly they decry the problem with illegal immigration, make no mistake, if any amnesty program was passed into law, the unions would all stampede to the new membership trough in order to secure more union dues. They would attempt to sell such betrayal to the current union members as merely trying to make these workers' wages more in line with the current union members' wages in order to level the playing field. Many of the current members would buy that argument completely. Even the members that did not buy it would be helpless to do anything, as they have seniority on their jobs. What could they do?

Temperatures would rise; however, after a brief period of time, the senior members would quiet down and go back to the business of earning money for their respective families. The unions would continue to make hay with their members by complaining about the building of factories in these Latin American countries. No one would notice that next to the illegal immigrant, the unions would have gained the most through any amnesty program. The members would have been duped, and many would not even know it. They would have fought against the "exportation of jobs to Latin American countries," only to lose those same jobs here in the United States to illegal immigrants that were granted amnesty and were now unionized. Although many will rightfully claim it is not our responsibility to do it and doing so will hurt American workers, we have a vested interest as a nation to help build the Latin American countries' economies. If we do not, we will never quell the flood of illegal immigrants to the United States; this will hurt not only those same workers, but also many others workers as well.

The problem of illegal immigration is that it is indeed a multi-headed monster. There is no quick fix; it will be costly to the taxpayers either through enforcement or through acquiescence.

Disgruntlement #11:
WE WILL BURY OURSELVES

Nikita Krushchev, November 19, 1956: "We will bury you." The quote was to imply that communism would outlive capitalism. While capitalism is alive and well in the United States, there are many that move incrementally towards a communist state. The doctrine of "from each according to his ability, to each according to his need" (Karl Marx, 1875) is also alive and well. Currently, the government funds the needs of many of the impoverished by supplying them with food stamps, welfare checks, and government housing.

When they grow too old to provide for themselves, the government provides them with Medicare and Social Security checks. This is achieved by taxing the middle and upper classes (the able-to-pay group) to afford the provisions for the poor. (The need–to-be-provided-for group). Already, the die has been cast. This is all done in the name of humanity and decency. Many citizens will think this is all funded from the upper class, and many politicians will hang their hats on this distortion of the truth. As they parade around victoriously as having stuck it to the wealthy, they will have instead stuck it to the middle class. The gap between the middle class and upper class widens because of programs designed to stick it to the upper class. It actually pushes more people from the middle class back into poverty, creating an even broader base of impoverished and an even larger amount of people relying on the government. Currently, through the campaign for the 2008 presidential election, we have some candidates that would further that government dependence by requiring America's citizens to be provided with government health care. This will be done in the name of humanity and decency as well. This would mean another massive expansion of government. Some in Congress think that government is to be all things to all people, another feather from the communist doctrine. This will, in essence, allow some people to never provide anything for their own well-being. Currently, in the United States, many impoverished live in a circle of poverty. There are those that do not finish high school and have children at an early age. Immediately they are entitled to WIC programs, food stamps, government housing, and health insurance for the children provided through the Children's Health Insurance Program (CHIPs). These children will be provided for by the government; many will then drop out of high school and have more children and start the circle all over again. The government continues to provide entitlements with little help in improving education in our schools. The government can only perpetuate the cycle with these entitlements; they cannot break it without providing better schools and better teachers. If they did provide a better educational opportunity, then individuals could break the cycle themselves. As was noted in "Disgruntlement #4: Today's Youth," we cannot improve on the education of our youth by reducing the authority of the faculty in our schools, nor the authority of the parents in our households. When we do not educate our youth, we sentence them to a life of poverty and despair. We also reduce them to a life of awaiting the government handout, like a beggar on the street.

Taking a closer look at CHIPs: CHIPs is simply Medicaid for children. You will find more government bureaucracy when the individual states stick their hands into disbursement of funds. Medicaid is a program that is paid by the federal government, but administered by each state government. The following is a true story about a man who had a son with special needs. For a short time, his youngest son was on Medicaid. His son was born with many birth defects and has had many surgeries to correct this affliction. He lives in Mississippi, approximately four miles from Louisiana. For years, his son had been going to Children's Hospital in New Orleans, Louisiana; this hospital is approximately one hour from his home and is an excellent children's hospital with an excellent staff. His insurance from his employer covered most of the medical expenses. However, after he changed employers and Medicaid was all the insurance he had for his son, he got his education on government-administered insurance. He was told that many doctors in Louisiana would not accept Mississippi Medicaid. Although the hospital would be more than happy to process Medicaid claims from any state, they had no control over a doctor's billing practices. He was flabbergasted. He told the doctors that it was a federal government program and he did not understand why there was a problem. Finally, after talking with several doctors at one of his son's consults, his son's dentist at the consult explained it to him. The dentist advised him that he, the dentist, had two practices—one in Mississippi and one in Louisiana. The dentist further advised him that the Mississippi practice did not accept Louisiana Medicaid and the Louisiana practice did not accept Mississippi Medicaid for the following reason and the following reason only: the dentist said, "Medicaid always pays less than normal insurance. However, unlike a medical claim that is paid by a normal insurance company, wherein the patient is responsible for the balance, an acceptance from a Medicaid payment requires the doctor or medical institution to hold the patient harmless of any balance not paid by Medicaid. Furthermore, when a medical claim is paid outside of the state, the state, administrators can reduce the Medicaid payment even further." The dentist continued, saying that he once billed a claim out of the wrong office. His billing staff sent the claim from the wrong state. His bill was for $125. Instead of receiving a payment from Louisiana Medicaid for $80, he received payment from Mississippi Medicaid for $16. All states do this in order to keep the Medicaid money inside the state. The federal government allows this, provided the states follow the federal statutes in administering the program. For the typical cold or stomachache, this would be an understandable policy. However, the father was living in Biloxi, Mississippi, when his son was born. He and his wife were sent to Children's and Women's Hospital in Mobile, Alabama, approximately one hour from where he lived, when his son was born. This was necessary due to the nature of the baby's birth defects; the doctors were already aware that the baby would need a more specialized hospital. After the baby was born, the baby stayed at Children's and Women's Hospital for two weeks; he was then sent to the Ochsner Foundation Hospital in New Orleans for a surgery. There were no hospitals on the Mississippi Gulf coast that could give the needed care for his son.

After coming to the realization that his son would no longer be going to Chlidren's Hospital in New Orleans, Louisiana, it was necessary that he drive almost three hours to a children's hospital in Jackson, Mississippi. Concisely, if a child in Southhaven, Mississippi, had cancer, Mississippi Medicaid would not pay St. Jude's Children's Hospital in Memphis as much money as it would the Children's Hospital in Jackson, Mississippi. The difference is between a one-mile drive to Memphis, Tennessee, and a three-and-a-half-hour drive to Jackson, Mississippi. All this because of government bureaucracy. It must be noted that many, if not all, states engage in this practice. It appears that they operate this as well as they do social security.

If the government provides health care for all, the price of medical care will not go down. The government will have to tax more than what is needed because it wastes so much of the money on pork-barrel programs. Taxes on the middle class, as well as the upper class, will go up. The poor pay no tax, the upper class will head for the tax shelters, and the middle class will be standing there holding the bag. The government currently taxes alcohol and tobacco as "sin" taxes. They have, in the last few years, raised taxes on tobacco, under the excuse that it is unhealthy and they are trying to curtail smoking in the hope of promoting good health. What happens when they cannot raise enough money from tobacco? This will eventually happen when the price becomes higher than the consumer can afford, or simply that the consumer refuses to pay the price. Perhaps unhealthy fast food is next. Maybe a Big Mac or Whopper will cost $10 each. The liberals have pushed the fact that cigarettes are unhealthy, and it drives the cost of healthcare up for everyone. How long before they push the same claim for obesity driving health care cost up for everyone? The crusade against cigarettes began with consumer lawsuits against tobacco companies. We have already started to see legal action against the fast-food industry. Many think there is nothing to this, probably the same ones that thought there was nothing to the initial lawsuits against tobacco companies.

We have cast aside the words of John F. Kennedy; "Ask not what your country can do for you, but you can do for your country." We are inching closer and closer to becoming a state in which the government provides all the needs of its people, while taxing the citizens that work to pay for their own responsibilities. The targets of many fascist governments in the past were the poor of those countries. This is where discontent is bred. This is fertile ground for politicians to promise anything. The citizens of this country need to stand up ask what price must be paid. How much is your freedom worth? Unfortunately, these questions will not be asked as people rush unknowingly, ready to give up what no country has ever been able to take from us. They will not be happy once they have relinquished their freedom and responsibility anymore than they are happy today; the only difference is they will be powerless to do anything about it. There will be no Daniel Webster to get us out of the deal we made with the Devil. We will have buried ourselves.

ABOUT THE AUTHOR

U.S. Army veteran, born in Indianapolis, IN., Raised in a small town in the state of Mississippi. As a former single father of four young boys I dealt with the day to day stress of raising a family and working long hours. Happily married now for five years, with a larger family of 10 children. I have always sought to set a good example for my children and others by trying to grasp everything life has to offer. As an outside salesman for 20 years combined with my travels in the military, I have had the opportunity to meet and discuss various issues with everyday people from all over the country. These issues, I have sought to expound on, so that others may know their frustrations are not isolated to them as individuals.